THE POLITICS OF IDEAS

DEEPAK

BLUEROSE PUBLISHERS
India | U.K.

Copyright © Deepak 2024

All rights reserved by author. No part of this publication may be reproduced, stored in a retrieval system or transmitted in any form or by any means, electronic, mechanical, photocopying, recording or otherwise, without the prior permission of the author. Although every precaution has been taken to verify the accuracy of the information contained herein, the publisher assume no responsibility for any errors or omissions. No liability is assumed for damages that may result from the use of information contained within.

BlueRose Publishers takes no responsibility for any damages, losses, or liabilities that may arise from the use or misuse of the information, products, or services provided in this publication.

For permissions requests or inquiries regarding this publication,
please contact:

BLUEROSE PUBLISHERS
www.BlueRoseONE.com
info@bluerosepublishers.com
+91 8882 898 898
+4407342408967

ISBN: 978-93-6783-099-4

Cover design: Daksh
Typesetting: Tanya Raj Upadhyay

First Edition: October 2024

This book is dedicated to my grandparents

HISTORICAL BACKGROUND

We have no complete writings from any of the Pre-Socratics, and from some, nothing at all. Our sources, then, are primarily twofold: fragments and testimonia. The fragments are purported bits of the thinkers' actual words. These might be fragments of books that they wrote or simply recorded sayings. In any case, there are no surviving complete works from the Pre-Socratics. Moreover, it is important to remember that there are no original compositions of any length or degree of completeness available. Neither, for that matter, are any originals available from Plato or Aristotle. In the pre-printing press days, scribes copied whatever editions of books and other written works they had available. We have texts that have been copied many times over. This means that, even with the fragments, we can never be sure whether the words we are reading correspond exactly to the original ideas expressed by the Pre-Socratics.

The ancient testimonies come to us from several sources, each with its own agenda and degree of reliability. Both Plato and Aristotle explicitly name many of the Pre-Socratics, sometimes discussing their supposed ideas at length. We must recognize that both philosophers almost certainly treated Pre-Socratic thought in light of their own respective philosophical agendas. Therefore, the information we get from them about the Pre-Socratics is likely skewed and sometimes arrantly false. Plato wrote philosophical literary dialogues and likely needed to represent the Pre-Socratics in his own peculiar ways to meet the needs of these dialogues. Aristotle, who wrote in the treatise style to which we are more accustomed today, also references the Pre-Socratics in the context of his own philosophy.

Table of Contents

1. Bias of Priene 1
2. Chilon of Sparta 5
3. Cleobulus of Lindos 8
4. Periander of Corinth 11
5. Pittacus of Mytilene 14
6. Solon of Athenes 18
7. Thales 22
8. Anaximander 34
9. Anaximenes 42
10. Xenophanes 52
11. Heraclitus 58
12. Parmenides 64
13. Zeno of Elea 71
14. Empedocles 80
15. Anaxagoras 92
16. Leucippus and Democritus 97
17. Sophists 104
18. Socrates 114

Bias was a poet, philosopher and statesman widely renowned for his rhetorical skills and his strong sense of justice. He was one of the Seven Sages of Ancient Greece who flourished in Priene during the 6th century BCE. His biography was written by Diogenes Laertius. As a judge, he would take only just cases. As a poet, he wrote a poem composed of 2,000 lines, along with numerous others that have been lost. As a statesman, Bias was never actually involved with politics on a practical scale. Nevertheless, he was involved in the salvation of his country from its siege by Alyattes, king of Lydia, using an ingenious trick, that he came up with, to outwit the king. In addition, he served as advisor to kings and generals concerning administrative and strategic subjects matters.

Bias is most renowned today for his sayings, which reflect his wisdom and sense of justice. Perhaps his most famous one is «Οἱ πλεῖστοι ἄνθρωποι κακοί» (Most men are evil). For this reason, Bias considered democracy an unsuitable political system. Other of his sayings include:

- «Ἀnclude ἄncla μ μlίνει διι πλoλo δ» – Do not honor the rich if he is a man without values.
- «Ἄ the πολλά» – Listen to many.
- «Βραδέως ἐδέως ς · ἕως ςἃ ἃ ἕω, διαβεβαιοιοιοτο manymanynyn without valuese political system.
- «Κττβαι ἐι μμ νεότητι εεπραξίαν, ἐρ δδ ττ γήρρ σοφίαν. Ἔν. α ἔν. μνήμην, καιρκ εεκαβειαν, τρόπρόγενναιότητα, πόνό ἑνότητα,αν, φόβόβεόβ βειαν, πλούτν φιλίαν, λόγ πειθώ, σιγι κόσμον, γνώμώ δικαιοσύνην, τόλμύ ἀόλμύναν, πράξει δυναστείαν, δόξε ἡόξείαναν» – In your youth, seek to earn the means of a comfortable life; in your old age, wisdom. With your work, you will acquire memory; with circumstances, respect; with your behavior, bravery; with your efforts, temperance; with your fears, euseby; with wealth, friendship; with logos, persuasion; with silence, ornaments; with mind, justice; with boldness, gallantry; with your actions, power; with your good name, authority.

- «Φρόνησιν ἀρόπα» – Love prudence.
- «Πείσας λάβε, με βιασάμενος» – Accept of things, having procured them by persuasion, not by force.
- «Λάλει καίρια» – Speak when the time is right.
- «Ὅ,τι ἂτ ἀταθι Sράσσ S, θεούς. μ σεαυτυττ ἰυτυ» – Whatever good fortune befalls you, attribute it to the gods.

It is said that Bias died in old age in the court during the pleading of one of his clients. The epitaph on his tomb, as quoted by Diogenes Laertius, reads:

Beneath this stone lies Bias, who was born in the illustrious Prienian land, The glory of the whole Ionian race.

Bias was the son of Teutamus and a citizen of Priene. Satyrus regarded him as the wisest of all the Seven Sages of Greece. One of the examples of his goodness is the legend that says he paid a ransom for some women who had been taken prisoner. After educating them as his own daughters, he sent them back to Messina, their homeland, and to their fathers.

Also, it is said that when some fishermen found The Brazen Tripod, on which was encrypted "For the Wisest", the fathers of the damsels held an assembly. They concluded that Bias was the wisest among all men, so the tripod was presented to him as a token of gratitude for all that he had done for the city. Bias refused the honour with the words, "Apollo is the wisest". Another author notes that he consecrated the tripod at Thebes to Hercules.

He also wrote about two thousand verses on Ionia, to show in what manner a man might achieve happiness. Some of his sayings were:

- "All men are wicked."
- "It is difficult to bear a change of fortune for the worse with magnanimity."
- "Choose the course which you adopt with deliberation; but when you have adopted it, then persevere in it with firmness."

- "Do not speak fast, for that shows folly."
- "Love prudence."
- "Speak of the Gods as they are."
- "Do not praise an undeserving man because of his riches."
- "Accept of things, having procured them by persuasion, not by force."
- "Cherish wisdom as a means of traveling from youth to old age, for it is more lasting than any other possession."

Bias left no written record, but much is known of his views. He was very skeptical, famously saying that most people are bad. He was also a representative thinker with an emphasis on piety, temperance, good manners, etc. He was also very charitable.

When Priene was attacked by the Persians, all the inhabitants fled, trying to take as many valuables as possible. Only Bias carried nothing, because he said that he carried everything important with him. He considered knowledge to be the most important.

Chilon of Sparta, or Chilo of Sparta, was a Lacedaemonian, son of Damagetus, and one of the Seven Sages of Greece. As an ephor (556 BCE), he strengthened that position in Sparta. It is recorded that he composed verses in elegiac metre to the number of two hundred. Chilon was also the first person who introduced the custom of joining the ephors to the kings as their counselors, though Satyrus attributes this institution to Lycurgus.

Some of his sayings:

- "Do not speak evil of the dead."
- "Honor old age."
- "Prefer punishment to disgraceful gain; for the one is painful but once, but the other for one's whole life."
- "Do not laugh at a person in misfortune."
- "If one is strong, be also merciful, so that one's neighbors may respect one rather than fear one."
- "Learn how to regulate one's own house well."
- "Do not let one's tongue outrun one's sense."
- "Restrain anger."
- "Do not dislike divination."
- "Do not desire what is impossible."
- "Do not make too much haste on one's road."
- "Obey the laws."

Chilon flourished around the beginning of the 6th century BCE. The tradition was that he died of joy in the arms of his son, who had just won a prize at the Olympic games.

Chilon of Sparta added his dictum to the precepts of the Seven Sages: "Don't desire that which is impossible."

In the face of insurmountable odds—
your hesitation to commit to me
and my pressing want for a spouse and child—

I decided to heed this wisdom of old
and bury my wishful love for you and
my stubborn hope for us deep within—

like the photo of a broken couple,
taken down from the bedroom wall and placed
under papers in a seldom-used drawer.

There, may time preserve the good that was us
and set the bit of you that is in me
into a memory of unspoiled joy,

or, at least, keep it from gathering dust
and losing all of its luster so that
years from now, when I'm rummaging around,

in search of one thing or another else,
I don't come upon it on a back shelf
and wonder why I felt it worth keeping.

Caption: 17th century illustration of Chilon (6th century BCE), Spartan philosopher and one of the Seven Sages of Greece. Chilon was one of the elected governors, or ephors, of Sparta who advised the king. As a thinker, he wrote many elegiac poems that contained sayings and aphorisms we still use today, such as "Do not speak ill of the dead" and "Do not laugh at a person in misfortune." As a statesman, he is credited with the militarisation of Sparta and thus its strength and influence in later centuries.

Cleobulus was born in the 7th century and he was the son of Evagoras. He was also a citizen or resident of Lindos in Rhodes. He became the ruler of Lindos City for more than 40 years. Cleobulus also went to Egypt to study philosophy, and it was said that he was a remarkable power. His daughter, named Cleobulina, also became an established poet of her time. Besides his fame as the most righteous ruler, he was the author of songs and riddles, making more than 3000 lines in all. Some people spoke of Cleobulus very highly. In fact, many important figures called Cleobulus as the King of the Lindians. He was also thought to be a nice and strong person. He was also dubbed as "The Wise" and was recognized as one of the Seven Sages of Greece.

Cleobulus and His Legacy

Cleobulus is believed to have lived until the age of 70 . If you visit Lindos, you can see a huge stone on the peninsula opposite the Acropolis of Lindos. This stone is called the Tomb of Cleobulus, and it is a very beautiful setting that offers a scenic view of Lindos village. However, it is said that this is not really where Cleobulus was buried in the first place. Nonetheless, a walk to this place is definitely one of the must things to do when you are in Lindos.

However, this site remains to be a very wonderful homage to Cleobulus because during his time of reigning, it was believed that Lindos thrived. It was also said that Cleobulus was the one responsible for the success and wealth of Lindos when he was in command of the place during 6th century BCE.

One more significant homage to Cleobulus is an asteroid that was named in his memory. There was an asteroid discovered in 1989 and this was called 4503 Cleobulus. There were also many sayings that were attributed to him.

So, the next time you decide to take a trip to Lindos, make sure that you don't only visit the sites and attractions but also commemorate the people who played important roles in them, such as Cleobulus.

After his death, an inscription was made that reads:

"Here the wise rhodian, Cleobulus, sleeps, and o'er his ashes sea - proud lindus we."

Cleobulus most famous sayings

- "Ignorance and talkativeness bear the chief sway among men."
- "Cherish not a thought."
- "Do not be fickle or ungrateful."
- "Be fond of hearing rather than of talking."
- "Be fond of learning rather than unwilling to learn."
- "Seek virtue and eschew vice."
- "Be superior to pleasure."
- "Instruct one's children."
- "Be ready for reconciliation after quarrels."
- "Avoid injustice."
- "Do nothing by force."
- "Moderation is the best thing."

Periander, son of Cypselus, ruled Corinth for more than 40 years. He was considered one of the Seven Sages of Greece. He restricted the number of slaves in Corinth, trying to keep the citizens busy in order to prevent them from conspiring against him. He greatly supported the arts, constructing various buildings, and tried to cut a naval passage through the Isthmos. However, he was prevented by the Delphic Oracle, who warned him not to proceed. The real reason, that he did not try though, was that such a giant project was above the technical capabilities of his time. Instead, he constructed the Diolcos, a stone road that allowed ships to be carried on wheeled platforms from the eastern port of Cenchreae in the Saronic gulf to the western port of Lechaeon in the Corinthian gulf. Periander founded new colonies for Corinth such as Naucratis in Egypt. He brought economic wealth in Corinth, the arts flourished, as well crafts and architecture.

Writing and philosophy

Periander was said to be a patron of literature, known for both writing and appreciating early philosophy. He is said to have written a didactic poem 2,000 lines long. In *Lives and Opinions of Eminent Philosophers*, Diogenes Laertius points out that writers disagree on who the Seven Sages are. It is posited that Periander tried to improve order in Corinth. Although he appears on Diogenes Laertius's list, his extreme measures and despotic gestures make him more suited to a list of famous tyrants than of wise men.

Rule

Periander built Corinth into one of the major trading centers in Ancient Greece. He established colonies at Potidaea in Chalcidice and Apollonia in Illyria, conquered Epidaurus, formed positive relationships with Miletus and Lydia, and annexed Corcyra, where his son lived much of his life. He is also credited with inventing a transport system, the Diolkos, across the Isthmus of Corinth. Tolls from goods entering Corinth's port accounted for nearly all the government revenues, which Periander used to build temples and other public works and to promote literature and the arts. He invited the poet Arion from Lesbos to Corinth for an arts festival in the city. Periander held many festivals and built numerous buildings in the Doric style. The Corinthian style of pottery was developed by an artisan during his rule.

Periander's style of leadership and politics was termed a 'tyranny'. Tyrants favoured the poor over the rich, sometimes confiscating landlord's possessions and enacting laws that limited their privileges. They also started the construction of temples, ports and fortifications, and improved the drainage of the city and supply of water. Periander adopted measures that benefitted commerce.

Influences

Periander is referenced by many contemporaries in relation to philosophy and leadership. Most commonly he is mentioned as one of the Seven Sages of Ancient Greece, a group of philosophers and rulers from early Greece, but some authors leave him out of the list. In Lives and Opinions of Eminent Philosophers, Diogenes Laertius, a philosopher of the 3rd century AD, lists Periander as one of these Seven Sages. Ausonius also refers to Periander as one of the Sages in his work *The Masque of the Seven Sages*.

Some scholars have argued that the ruler named Periander was a different person from the sage of the same name. Diogenes Laertius writes that "Sotion, Heraclides, and Pamphila in the fifth book of her Commentaries say that there were two Perianders; one a tyrant, and the other a wise man, native of Ambracia. Neanthes of Cyzicus makes the same assertion, adding that the two men were cousins to one another. Aristotle says that it was the Corinthian Periander who was the wise one; but Plato contradicts him.

Pittacus was the son of Hyrradius and one of the Seven Sages of Greece. He was a native of Mytilene and a Mytilenaean general who, with his army, was victorious in the battle against the Athenians and their commander Phrynon. In consequence of this victory, the Mytilenaeans held Pittacus in the greatest honour and presented the supreme power into his hands. After ten years of reign, he resigned his position, and the city and constitution were brought into good order.

When the Athenians were about to attack his city, Pittacus challenged their General to a single combat, with the understanding that the result should decide the war, and much bloodshed be thereby avoided. The challenge was accepted, and he killed his enemy with a broadsword. He was then chosen as the ruler of his city and governed for ten years, during which he made laws in poetry—one of which stated, "A crime committed by a person when drunk should receive double the punishment it would merit if the offender were sober." His great motto was: "Do not do to your neighbor what you would take ill from him" (The Golden Rule).

Some authors mention that he had a son called Tyrrhaeus. The legend says that his son was killed, and the murderer was brought before Pittacus, he dismissed the man, saying, "Pardon is better than repentance." Of this matter, Heraclitus says that he had got the murderer into his power and then he released him, saying, "Pardon is better than punishment."

It was a saying of Pittacus that it is a hard thing to be a good man. Plato in his *Protagoras* has Socrates discuss this saying at length with Protagoras and has Prodicus of Ceos call the Aeolic dialect that Pittacus spoke barbarian: "He didn't know to distinguish the words correctly, being from Lesbos and raised with a barbarian dialect."

TYRANT

Pittacus of Mytilene was a general from the island of Lesvos and one of the Seven Sages of ancient Greece. Essentially an autodidact, he was revered for his military might, political prudence, and wisdom. He governed Mytilene for 10 years, establishing himself as one of the most important historical figures of the island and of Greek history.

Pittacus first entered politics when he cooperated with the two brothers of Alcaeus, Cicys and Antimenidas, the representatives of the aristocracy, to kill the Lesvian tyrant Melagchron and take over as the new ruler of Lesvos. A few years later, he was elected general of his peoples in the war against Athens. In the battle for Sigeion, a harbour in Hellispontus was controlled by the Athenians. Pittacus challenged their general Phrynon, an Olympian in pankration, to a duel, whom he killed. Sigeion returned to Lesvian rule, and Pittacus was honoured with a portion of land, for which he agreed to receive only the size equal to the distance where his javelin would reach. This part of land became known as "Land of Pittacus".

After a series of political upheavals, Pittacus was granted complete power over Lesvos, serving as general for a second time from 595 BCE to 579 BCE. Thus, he ruled in a system of "appointive tyranny" (αἰρετὴ τυραννίς), which differed from the barbaric tyranny in that it was not based on heritage but resembled monarchy, as the dictator was elected by the people.

As tyrant of Lesvos, Pittacus reformed the laws, changing the old legislation concerning monarchy, and granted amnesty to all exiled political rivals of the government. After ruling prudently for over a decade, Pittacus resigned willingly from his position as tyrant and died a few years later. By the time of his resignation, he had achieved fame throughout Greece due to his wisdom and was visited by those seeking to hear his advice.

SAYINGS

None of Pittacus's works have survived, but multiple quotes have been saved by Diogenes Laertius and Stobaeus attributed to Pittacus. Of those, following are some of the most well-known:

- «Συγγνώμη μετανοίας κρείσσων». – "Forgiveness is better than pertinence." Another variant of the quote was "Forgiveness is better than revenge."
- «Ἄνδρα ἀγαθὸν ἀλαθέως γενέσθαι χαλεπόν». – "It is difficult for man to be genuinely good."
- «'Ανάγκα δ' οὐδὲ θεοὶ μάχονται». – "Not even Gods can resist necessity."
- «Ἀρχὴ ἄνδρα δεικνύει». – "Power proves the man."
- «Τὰς νίκας ἄνευ αἵματος ποιεῖσθαι». – "Achieve victories without blood."
- «Σωφροσύνην φιλεῖν.» – "Love sophrosyne."
- «Συνετῶν ανδρῶν εἶναι, πρὶν γενέσθαι τὰ δυσχερῆ προνοῆσαι ὅπως μὴ γένηται, ἀνδρείων δὲ γενόμενα εὖ θέσθαι». – "It is for wise men to foresee, before the difficult things come, so that they do not happen; it is for the brave to face them, should they happen."

Solon, a prominent Athenian statesman, lawmaker, and poet, played an essential role in the development of democracy in Ancient Greece. He lived during a time of significant political and social unrest in Athens. Solon's astute political maneuvering and reforms laid the groundwork for the establishment of democracy, and he is remembered as one of the Seven Sages of Greece.

Early Life and Career

Born into a wealthy Athenian family, Solon was well-educated and belonged to the elite circles of society. His early life was marked by his interest in poetry and philosophy, through which he often conveyed his thoughts on politics and social issues. Despite his privileged upbringing, Solon was deeply concerned about the widespread social and economic inequalities plaguing Athens.

Athenian Society in Crisis

During the 7th century BCE, Athens was facing a severe economic crisis, fueled by widespread debt bondage, unequal land distribution, and the exploitation of the lower classes by the aristocracy. As tensions mounted, the Athenians sought a leader who could bring about social and political stability. Solon, known for his wisdom, fairness, and diplomatic skills, emerged as the ideal candidate to address the mounting crisis.

Solon's Reforms

In 594 BCE, Solon was appointed as the Archon, the chief magistrate of Athens, and was tasked with implementing crucial reforms to address the social and economic issues. His sweeping reforms, known as the Seisachtheia or "Shaking off of Burdens," transformed Athenian society and laid the foundation for the democratic system that would later emerge.

Solon's key reforms included:

- **Debt Relief**: Solon cancelled all debts, which freed numerous Athenians from debt bondage and restored confiscated lands to their original owners.
- **Constitutional Reforms**: He restructured the political system, giving all male citizens the right to participate in the Athenian Assembly and law courts, irrespective of their wealth or social status.
- **Economic Reforms**: Solon encouraged trade, promoted the growth of industries, and introduced standardized coinage, which helped revive the Athenian economy.
- **Legal Reforms**: He instituted a new legal code, replacing the draconian laws of Draco, and established a more equitable legal system.

Solon's travels after Athens

After implementing his reforms in Athens, Solon left the city for a self-imposed period of exile. The exact reasons for his departure remain unclear, but it is believed that he left to avoid potential unrest or backlash as his reforms took effect. During his exile, Solon traveled extensively, visiting places such as Egypt, Cyprus, and Lydia. One notable encounter during Solon's travels was with the Lydian King Croesus in his capital city, Sardis. Their conversation, preserved by the ancient Greek historian Herodotus, is a famous tale of wisdom and hubris. In their exchange, Croesus asked Solon who the happiest person was, expecting Solon to praise his immense wealth and power. However, Solon responded by highlighting the fates of three individuals who had led virtuous lives and died with honor. This answer served as a reminder that true happiness and prosperity should not be judged by wealth and power alone, but by one's actions and character.

His long-term impacts

Though not all of Solon's reforms were successful, and some were even reversed after his death, his work left a lasting impact on Athenian society and the evolution of democracy. His reforms laid the groundwork for the later democratic reforms of Cleisthenes, which led to the birth of the Athenian democracy we know today. Solon's ideas on governance, social justice, and the rule of law have resonated throughout the centuries, influencing not only the development of democratic principles in ancient Greece but also shaping the foundations of modern Western political thought.

Solon's legacy as a lawmaker, statesman, and poet continues to inspire and inform our understanding of democracy and social justice. By recognizing the importance of political inclusiveness and the rule of law, Solon's work serves as a reminder of the essential principles that underpin democratic societies today.

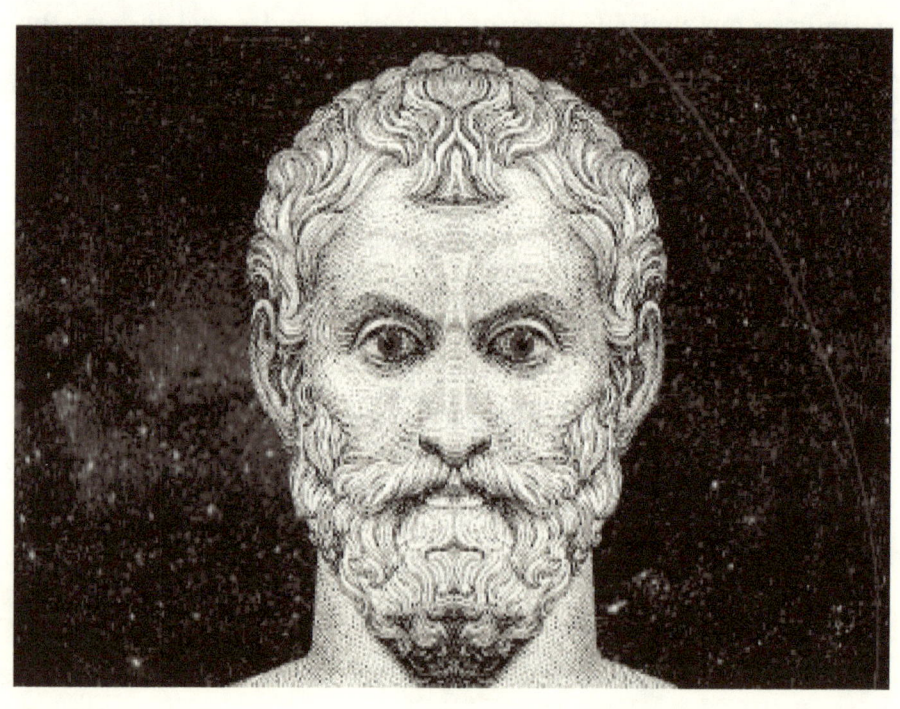

Thales of Miletus was one of the seven sages of antiquity. The ancient Greek philosopher Thales was born in Miletus in Greek Ionia. Aristotle, the major source for Thales's philosophy and science, identified Thales as the first person to investigate the basic principles and the question of the originating substances of matter. Therefore, he is considered as the founder of the school of natural philosophy. Thales looked for patterns in nature to explain the way the world worked rather than believing everything happened solely because one of the Greek gods commanded it. He replaced superstitions with science.

Thales was interested in almost everything and investigated almost all areas of knowledge including philosophy, history, science, mathematics, engineering, geography, and politics. He proposed theories to explain many of the events of nature, identified the primary substance, the support of the earth, and the cause of change. Thales was much involved in the problems of astronomy and provided a number of explanations for the cosmological events which traditionally involved supernatural entities. His questioning approach to the understanding of heavenly phenomena was the beginning of Greek astronomy. Thales' hypotheses were new and bold, and in freeing phenomena from godly intervention, he paved the way towards scientific endeavour. He founded the Milesian school of natural philosophy, developed the scientific method, and initiated the first Western enlightenment. Many anecdotes are closely connected to Thales' investigations of the cosmos.

When considered in association with his hypotheses they take on added meaning and are most enlightening. Thales was highly esteemed in ancient times, and a letter cited by Diogenes Laertius, and purporting to be from Anaximenes to Pythagoras, advised that all our discourse should begin with a reference to Thales. There may have been other scientists before Thales, but if there were we do not know their names. Today, Thales is widely accepted as the first philosopher in the Western tradition. Although some of his concepts, like the idea that everything is made of water, seem out of place in the 21st century

Thales and Monopoly

"...it is easy for philosophers to be rich if they choose, but this is not what they care about."

In a story told by Aristotle, Thales of Miletus provided one of the best arguments in defense of the life of a philosopher. In this story, Thales observed the celestial bodies and managed to predict that the next crop of olives would be unusually productive. He then invested in the olive presses of Miletus and Chios. When the olives were ready to be turned to olive oil, he controlled the rate in which they were brought. This way he made a huge profit. However, according to Aristotle, Thales did not do that in order to make money but to prove that a philosopher could live a wealthy life if they chose to. This way Thales gave an answer to everyone who called his profession useless and made fun of his poverty. The Milesian proved that a philosopher is not poor by fate but by choice, at the same time signalling that there is a path of knowledge and spirituality offering higher satisfaction than the path of material wealth.

Aristotle was not convinced that this story was real. He thought that because of Thales's wisdom, people attributed him with the tactic of monopolising a market.

Early Life and Education

Thales was born into a privileged family in the ancient Greek city of Miletus around 624 BCE. His father's name was Examyes, and his mother's name was Cleobuline. He was born in the same era as Aesop, famous for his fables. When Thales was born, Miletus was one of the wealthiest and most powerful of all the Greek cities. Today it is located on the coast of Turkey. Thales was born into a Greek society that was intellectually less advanced than those to its east and south –such as the Babylonians and the Ancient Egyptians. The Babylonians were masterful astronomers and mathematicians, while the Egyptians were also far ahead of the Greeks in these fields.

In Egypt and Babylon, mathematics was used in commerce, astronomy, and construction projects; it was a thoroughly practical science. Astronomy was used to study the heavens to understand what the gods might be thinking. As a young man, Thales became a merchant, which was probably his family's line of business. In his later years, he travelled to Egypt, where he learned about astronomy and mathematics. He may have travelled to Babylon; if he did, it would have been during the reign of Nebuchadnezzar. When he returned to Miletus, he changed careers, took a big drop in income, and became Ancient Greece's first scientist.

JACK OF ALL TRADES

Not much is known about his life, but he was revered as one of the wisest Greeks of all time. He was included in the list of the seven sages of antiquity by Plato and was considered to be the first philosopher by Aristotle. Traditionally, Thales is always listed as the first Presocratic philosopher. He is part of the group of the Milesian philosophers including Anaximander and Anaximenes, who were his students and continuers of his thinking. In addition, due to his belief that everything derives from one and only element, water, he is also a monist philosopher just like the rest of the Milesians as well as the Ionian Greek philosopher Heraclitus.

Like most of the Presocratic philosophers, Thales was not simply a philosopher but rather a jack of all trades. He was a mathematician, an astronomer, and a mechanic. This was not something unusual. Science, theology, and philosophy were still deeply interconnected. At the time, a philosopher was a term used to signify someone who loved wisdom and knowledge in all its forms. The main difference of a presocratic Greek philosopher, like Thales, and an Egyptian priest of Osiris, a Persian magus, or a Buddhist mystic was the attempt to explain natural phenomena using natural principles. While Thales' view that everything derives from water can be traced back to Egyptian and Semitic creation myths, his theory was an attempt at explaining the material world using natural, and not theological, principles.

Diogenes Laertius, who lived in the third century CE, attributes the famous Delphic maxim "know thyself" to Thales, although the ancients disagree on this matter. In general, ancient sources disagree on whether Thales of Miletus ever wrote a book. In any case, the key ideas of his thought were preserved through the work of later philosophers and scholars.

DEATH

Thales' death is placed in the 550s, and there are two different versions of how he died. According to Apollodorus, he died of a heart stroke while watching the Olympic Games. However, Plato records that Thales was studying the stars of the night sky when he fell into a well. This story had a didactic value for the ancients warning them against spending too much time philosophizing, without caring about earthly matters.

However, the story could be a made-up legend. This was not uncommon in antiquity. Especially when it came to significant philosophers, politicians, and other influential personalities, the Greeks loved making up fake death stories that corresponded to the life or teachings of the deceased. Sometimes these stories were didactic and other times simply mean. In Thales' case, it was probably a combination of the two. In the story with the well, Thales died because he lost contact with the real world after being absorbed in his pursuit of higher knowledge. Making him drown in the well was also a fun way of dismissing his theory that everything is made of water.

TRAVELS TO EGYPT

"Thales... first went to Egypt and hence introduced this study [geometry] into Greece. He discovered many propositions himself and instructed his successors in the principles underlying many others, his method of attack being in some cases more general and in others more empirical."

It was quite common amongst the Greeks to credit their wisest with having visited Egypt. Pythagoras, Solon, and Plato are among the most notable examples. However, in the case of Thales of Miletus, it seems that he really visited the land of the Nile as many of his achievements, like the measuring of the pyramids' height, were set in Egypt. Even if Thales' visits never occurred, the legend may still point to the origins of the philosopher's ideas. Thales was surely aware of Egyptian views about the cosmos and its creation, but he managed to adapt them in a unique, unprecedented manner that led to the birth of philosophical thinking.

In addition, Geometry had originated in Egypt, and Egyptian mathematical knowledge was among the most advanced in the world. Without a doubt, this knowledge passed down to Thales who became known as the one who introduced Geometry to Greece.

The Philosophy of Thales

There are many types of monism, but Thales' philosophy can be classified as substance and materialist monism. Substance monism is the idea that everything in the world can be traced back to a single substance. For Thales of Miletus, this was water. Since he also appeared to believe that matter, in the form of water, was above abstract ideas, like the soul, he was also a materialist. The monism of Thales does not mean that Thales did not recognize the existence of other substances. It rather means that he held that the primary source of everything was to be found in water. Although this sounds preposterous today, Thales was onto something.

Water, the Origin of Everything

"Thales the Milesian doth affirm that water is the principle whence all things in the universe spring."

Thales believed that the world was made of water and that, at some point, everything would return to water. Today, we understand that water is the universal solvent and, as far as we can tell, a necessary component for the existence of life. Now imagine being a man looking for answers to the nature of things 2,600 years ago. As you are trying to reveal the mystery of existence, you make the following observation: water is everywhere. You find a vast ocean, rivers, lakes, rain, snow, and observe that every living organism depends on this one substance called water. After all this, you observe water in all its forms— liquid, solid, and gas. Water is absorbed into the earth, and earth into the sea.

This doesn't stop there. While you are looking for answers, you lean towards the ancient wisdom of Egyptian, Semitic, and, of course, Greek tales about the creation of the cosmos. What you discover there is a common pattern: water is highly revered as a force of regeneration. Even the most important Greek poet, Homer, considers gods of water, like Oceanus and Tethys, the parents of all gods.

"For I am faring to visit the limits of the all-nurturing earth, and Oceanus, from whom the gods are sprung, and mother Tethys…"

After all this, can you really blame Thales for thinking that water is the one and only substance out of which everything derives?

The Earth Floats on the Sea?

Thales believed that the earth floated on water. This was a conclusion he had drawn after he observed that the earth presented a solidity and immobility that the sea did not. Compatible with this view was also Thales' belief that earthquakes were caused by the oceans' roughness.

These ideas can also be traced back to Greek mythology, where the ocean god Poseidon was called "the Earth Shaker" and was considered to be the one responsible for earthquakes. Furthermore, there is debate as to whether Thales believed that the earth was flat or spherical. Although there are good reasons to suggest that Thales would have conceived the spherical shape of the earth through his astronomical endeavours, there is not sufficient evidence to back up this claim with certainty. Of course, it would not have been something preposterous for Thales to believe that the earth was round, as this was a common understanding among ancient Greek philosophers and astronomers.

Thales: The Science

At some point, after he returned to Miletus, Thales took a step beyond his teachers. (Of course, his teachers may have taken this step themselves, but if they did, there is no historical record of it.)

You Don't Need Hapi to Make the Nile Flood

In Egypt, the annual rise in the River Nile's level was vital for the success of the Kingdom's harvests. Every year, the silty river would rise and replenish the land around it with nutrients and moisture. The river would then fall, and Egyptians would farm the newly fertile land. Without the Nile, there could be no Kingdom of Egypt, because rain hardly ever fell there.

The Egyptians believed the Nile's floods were caused by Hapi, one of their many gods. If the gods were displeased, the river would not flood, and there would be famine. The gods had to be kept happy at all costs. Thales said that the Nile flooded for natural reasons, not because of Hapi. Nowadays, of course, we know the Nile floods because seasonal rains fall further south in Africa: in fact, it was another Ancient Greek, Eratosthenes, who was the first to figure this out, although Thales himself seems to have speculated about the true cause.

The switch between believing the gods were responsible for day-to-day events and believing that if we understood natural phenomena we could actually explain and predict events was Thales' greatest achievement. It unleashed people's ability to think about the underlying causes of what we observe. It was the first scientific thinking we know of: Thales was the man who dumped superstition in favour of science.

A nerd with his head in the clouds

One dark evening, Thales was out walking in Miletus, looking at the night sky. He stumbled into a ditch, whereupon an old woman, who knew him as a 'thinker' laughed and asked, "How can you see what the heavens are telling you when you can't even see what is under your own feet?"

Thales seems to have been Ancient Greece's first-ever academic – its first science nerd, in fact! He was mocked for it. In the wealthy city of Miletus, people told Thales that no one could ever prosper from merely thinking, and that's why he was not rich. Thales, however, proved his detractors wrong.

He had studied weather patterns in the region of Ionia, where the city of Miletus was located. The weather patterns one winter indicated that next season's olive harvest would be a bumper crop. While it was still winter, he placed small deposits to hire all the olive presses in Miletus for the next harvest. In summer, when the olive growers began to realise that a huge crop of olives was coming, they discovered Thales had hired all the olive presses.

Thales made a fortune by selling his rights to the presses to the olive growers. He carried out no physical work; he grew rich on mind power alone, applying his observations of weather patterns to predict how big the olive crop would be. He did not need any help from Aristaeus, the Greek god of olive groves.

Earthquakes

Ancient people believed earthquakes were a measure of their gods' anger. Sacrifices, including human sacrifices in some cultures, became the normal way of trying to pacify angry gods. Thales sought a rational explanation for earthquakes. He theorized that our whole planet Earth is a flat disk floating on an infinite sea of water and that earthquakes come when the planet is hit by a wave traveling through the water. With the benefit of modern science, we know Thales got it wrong. His theory was, however, an enormous advance on saying the earth shook because Zeus was annoyed about something. Thales had at least tried to find a rational explanation for earthquakes. A further benefit of Thales' ideas (mercifully) was they required no sacrifices to be made.

What Are Things Made Of?

Thales thought deeply about matter. He decided that, fundamentally, everything must be made of the same thing – much as today we believe that all matter is made of atoms. His idea was that in its most fundamental form, all matter is water. It took about 200 years for Thales' idea to be transformed by his compatriot Democritus into "all matter is atoms."

The Ancient Greek historian Plutarch, who lived 600 years after Thales, wrote that Egyptian priests claimed Thales' "everything is water" theory originally came out of Egypt.

Astronomy

Thales learned about astronomy in Egypt and possibly Babylon. When Archimedes was killed during the Roman conquest of Syracuse in 212 BC, the Roman historian Cicero wrote about the event. He tells us the Romans discovered Archimedes had a machine that accurately predicted the movement of the moon and planets and predicted solar and lunar eclipses. (Such a machine has actually been found by archeologists – it is an amazingly sophisticated device called the Antikythera Mechanism.) The Romans also found a more basic globe showing the celestial sphere – a forerunner of the Antikythera Mechanism – which had first been made by Thales.

Groundbreaking Mathematics

As with astronomy, Thales learned about mathematics in Egypt and possibly Babylon. Back in Miletus, he built on what he had learned and was the first person to use deductive logic in mathematics, producing new results in geometry. He established for the first time that mathematical theorems require proof before they are accepted as true.

He began transforming mathematics from a practical field of study to one that could be explored without worrying about practical applications.

Thus, Thales took great leaps towards modern pure mathematics, a subject based on deduction and proof, unconcerned about practical uses for its findings. (Funnily enough, although pure mathematics is performed with no thought for practical uses, discoveries in pure mathematics often turn out to be important in the real world!) Thales established the Milesian School, where he taught mathematics, setting the stage for mathematics to flourish in Ancient Greece.

Did Thales Believe in the Concept of Soul?

Thales of Miletus was a naturalist philosopher trying to explain the world by observing natural phenomena. He was a materialist thinker since he attributed everything to one element, water. Despite that, he seems to have believed in the concept of the soul too. According to Aristotle, Thales was the origin of the belief that the soul is a property of things that is to be found everywhere. This idea could have been the predecessor of Plato's concept of the soul.

"Thales, too, to judge from what is recorded about him, seems to have held the soul to be a motive force, since he said that the magnet has a soul in it because it moves the iron."

"Certain thinkers say that the soul is intermingled in the whole universe, and it is perhaps for that reason that Thales came to the opinion that all things are full of gods."

If we judge from these fragments, Thales did not even come close to Plato's idealism. Besides, his idea of the soul as a moving force of matter, at a first glance, appears closer to the idea of energy than the holy spirit in Christian theology. Of course, there are many ways to interpret these lines, and no way of knowing exactly what Thales said. In any case, it is more likely than not when Thales tried to make sense of reality, he found answers in a material substance, namely water, and not in god or an abstract idea.

The Heritage of Thales

Thales is the first person about whom we know to propose explanations of natural phenomena which were materialistic rather than mythological or theological. His theories were new, bold, exciting, comprehensible, and possible explanations. He did not speak in riddles as did Heraclitus and had no need to invent an undefined non-substance, as Anaximander did. Because he gave no role to mythical beings, Thales's theories could be refuted. Arguments could be put forward in attempts to discredit them. Thales's hypotheses were rational and scientific. Aristotle acknowledged Thales as the first philosopher and critiqued his hypotheses in a scientific manner.

The most outstanding aspects of Thales's heritage are: the search for knowledge for its own sake; the development of the scientific method; the adoption of practical methods and their development into general principles; his curiosity and conjectural approach to the questions of natural phenomena. In the sixth century B.C.E., Thales asked the question, 'What is the basic material of the cosmos?' The answer is yet to be discovered.

We might be familiar with the works of Aristotle, Socrates and Plato due to their contributions as early Greek scholars. But have you ever heard about Anaximander, the first philosopher to make massive changes to the astronomical world and to natural philosophy? He was a Pre-Socratic philosopher, so he predates the typical study of Greek scholars (that's probably why you never heard of him). Around 2,600 years ago, Anaximander became the first person in recorded history to recognize that the earth exists as a solitary body which does not need to rest on top of anything else. Fascinated by the structure of the earth, he produced one of the first ever maps of the world. He did not restrict his thinking to astronomy and geography. He also theorised about evolution, concluding that life had first arisen in wet rather than dry conditions. He proposed that the first humans had been produced from fish.

Beginnings

None of Anaximander's work survive, and what we know of him was written by authors, such as Aristotle. One of the most significant features of Anaximander's early life is that he was born in the city of Miletus. Now largely forgotten, at the time of Anaximander's birth, the city was booming. It had grown into the greatest and wealthiest city in Ancient Greece.

About 14 years before Anaximander was born, Miletus had been the birthplace of the first scientist in recorded history, Thales. In fact, Anaximander was possibly a blood relative of Thales.

The World's First Science Student

Anaximander was one of Thales' first students, perhaps the very first. Pythagoras was one of his later students. Pythagoras was also taught by Anaximander. Thales' core belief, which he passed to Anaximander, was that rational explanations, rather than the Ancient Greek gods should be used to account for natural phenomena.

1. Anaximander Invented a Proto-Evolutionary Human Anthropology

Anaximander had an unconventional idea about human beings. According to him, early life was first conceived inside water. This is now established as the premature prediction of evolution because of its correspondence with Charles Darwin's theory. However, Darwin figured this out 2000 years later. According to Anaximander's predecessor Thales, everything is fundamentally made out of water and hence that element serves as the origin of the universe. Anaximander takes this idea and resorts to it to explain the inception of humans. The Roman author Censorinus included Anaximander's theory in his own writings. Censorinus recounted Anaximander's thought as if he believed that actual fish-like creatures emerged from warmed-up water, and also the Earth itself. Men would take form inside these animals, while embryos were held prisoners until puberty. Only then, after these animals burst open out in nature, men and women could come out able to feed themselves. This theory was the cause of great debate among Greek scholars in the centuries that followed.

2. Introduction of Sundial And Earth's Shape

Anaximander's proposition of the Earth's floating nature in space dates back to 545 BCE. He did not believe in the presence of an absolute upwards or downwards force. This was in contrast to the ongoing theory proposed by Thales, which was formulated before Anaximander. Thales believed that the Earth was a flat disk, while Anaximander's hypothesis was that the Earth had a cylindrical shape. The progress from a 2D to a 3D shape was surely an upgrade, but it wasn't completely accurate. Among many of his other inventions, Anaximander was also responsible for introducing the sundial into Greek culture. He travelled to Sparta to set up a gnomon, a simple pillar that is fixed straight over markings on the ground, representing a dial. Based on the shadows cast by the pillar and their interaction with the markings, one could accurately tell the time.

3. The Genesis of Cosmic Body Ring

Anaximander supposed that the moon, sun and stars were not mere objects in space but wheels of fire that surrounded the Earth. According to him, these wheels do not move and remain stationary around the globe at all times. His portrayal of celestial bodies helped explain the detachment of the moon, stars and sun as far away from the Earth. This provided a well-defined explanation of the phases of the moon as well as its eclipses. These heavenly figures form after a fiery ring is encircled by air right after getting detached from the Earth's fire. An eclipse takes place if there is something blocking the holes through which the moon, stars, and sun shine, and are visible from the Earth. These holes are tubular pathways displaying the rings of fire. Anaximander's idea that the heavenly bodies move in a circular manner was certainly ahead of its time.

4. First Ever Mapping of the World

Anaximander is credited as the first Greek geographer to attempt the map of our world, at least according to ancient observers. It was not unusual to use regional maps in the olden times. However, the thought of mapping out the whole globe was much more novel. Only after Anaximander started this endeavour, Hecataeus of Miletus, who was a traveler, attempted making the perfect map out of his predecessor's creation while improving on it. Anaximander constructed maps of regions in the Black Sea. This map consisted of the Middle East along with regions corresponding to contemporary countries like Italy, Greece, Turkey, Egypt, Libya, and Israel. He devised this "global" map to improve trading, which concentrated around the Black Sea and toward Greek colonies, as well as Miletus. As Anaximander was a well-travelled man, he accumulated plenty of knowledge from his geographic expeditions to the Black Sea, Apollonia, as well as Sparta. Additional geographical coordinates were gathered from sailors who went to Miletus to stock up on merchandise.

5. The First Book On Natural Philosophy

Anaximander is the first scholar to write a book on Natural Philosophy, which paved the path for many contemporary philosophers. His book "On Nature" argued for the concept of the Apeiron. Most of this book is unidentified as the fragments are lost in time. A primary source is his successor, Theophrastus, who referenced some parts of "On Nature" and was a follower of Anaximander's accounts of Geography, Biology, and Astronomy. Anaximander's idea of the Apeiron has been discussed for millennia. Since Aristotle conveyed many of Anaximander's beliefs and hypotheses, he preserved another part of Anaximander's work: the idea of 'The Limitless'. He elaborates that the source of everything is to be fundamentally different from its creations and therefore unlimited as well. Even if something is responsible for the generation and destruction of everything, it cannot logically do this by itself; rather it has to be an unlimited entity — hence the Apeiron. The interesting point here is that Aristotle himself believed this idea to be rather absurd because he believed there was no logical justification of why the source of generation and destruction could not be limited. Poor reasoning or not, it is evident that the Apeiron played an important role in Anaximander's account of the creation of the universe.

6. Multiverse Theory and Parallel Universes

Anaximander had a broad view of multiverses back when few people had ever even considered the idea. His views on the matter matched those of Epicurus and Leucippus, as these philosophers were on the same page regarding the existence of parallel universes. These thinkers made great hypotheses about countless worlds which have different sizes, shapes, and natures in the universe, and that the objects within them move in endless motion inside the space vacuum. The idea was that the universe consists of a concentrated area with many globes on one side and planets scattered on the other side of it. Every world has a different paradigm of time and energy. Some planets might have a sun, while others just have the moon. Collisions are possible and could demolish the existence of any of the planets upon contact.

7. The Origin of Climatic Conditions

Anaximander proposed a theory of the formation of climatic phenomena such as lightning, thunder, winds and clouds. According to him, winds are the primary source of meteorological occurrences and carry out the processes of these atmospheric changes. Whirlwinds, lightning, thunder and typhoons take place when wind gets forced out of the clouds and causes a roar, bursting out with its full might. This then tears open the clouds and causes a flash to occur after suddenly rubbing against the thick clouds. All of this is impossible when the wind is "enclosed" in the cloud, and that is its natural state for the most part. This is why climatic conditions only rarely lead to extreme phenomena, and remain stable for the most part.

8. The Hovering Earth and Revolving Celestial Bodies

Anaximander changed the manner humans looked at the world forever. He asserted that celestial bodies move around the Earth in full circles. That seems apparent to us now but wasn't an obvious opinion back in Anaximander's time. He believed that the sun goes down while the moon comes up every day. Although we don't truly see where they go due to our limited consciousness; they just disappear and reappear later. Nevertheless, Anaximander asserts quite emphatically that things move in circles around the Earth and therefore pass underneath it. This thought leads to another idea: the Earth isn't resting on anything. There's nothing underneath it, nor is anything holding it upwards. If it were otherwise then the moon, sun and all the planets would not be able to circle the globe. Anaximander introduced another notion — that wasn't obvious in the ancient world — that heavenly bodies are spaced out at varying distances all over the galaxy. According to Homer, before Anaximander's proposition, people used to believe that the sky was a fixed surface above the earth. This is why Anaximander tried to work out the order of the celestial bodies but didn't quite get it right.

Regardless, he was successful in recognizing orbital spaces. This means that Anaximander is one of the first people to have conceived the idea of space itself.

9. A Cosmological Account of the Apeiron

Anaximander's concept of the Apeiron was deemed notoriously obscure and much more metaphysical than anything thought out by Thales, his predecessor. Many ancient works are dedicated to comprehending what the hell this Apeiron is! Aristotle preserves much of what we know about it but delivers conflicting definitions. Jonathan Barnes has even suggested that Anaximander himself did not know what this term actually meant. Regardless of these contrasting interpretations, it is known that Anaximander's Apeiron is spatially infinite, divine, eternal, and exists beyond the world we live in. What makes this concept of Apeiron so difficult to apprehend is that he does not specify the sort of substance this unlimited component was. Some scholars convey that Anaximander meant that this Apeiron had no determinate quality or was perhaps a mixture of elements. Others suggest that it was a bit like air. But setting that aside, we are dealing with an assumed primordial unlimited substance which is a source of the physical universe and that governs the law of nature. Anaximander characterised it by saying that it 'steers the cosmos like a ship.' The question arises: why did he posit this extraordinary thing? According to Anaximander, the material world is operated by opposing forces such as the wet versus the dry. In a rare fragment of Anaximander's writings, he says:

"Whence things have their origin, Thence also their destruction happens, According to necessity; For they give to each other justice and recompense For their injustice In conformity with the ordinance of Time."

By this, he meant that whenever a wet thing takes over a dry one, there is an injustice done to the dry entity which must be reciprocated with the dry body taking over the wet again, and so on and so forth. This interplay between opposites could go on indefinitely. Anaximander likely thought that the source of the opposites could not possess changing qualities and, because of this, that it had to be separate from the process it created.

Anaximander's Lasting Influence on the World

Anaximander is now universally recognized as a forward-thinking and influential philosopher. His views on cosmic occurrences and the explanations behind their trajectories was unique and, in some respects, predicted much of what we now know to be true.

Anaximander's work paved the way for modern astronomy by establishing fundamental concepts of the movements of the sun, moon and stars around the Earth. His knowledge pertaining to astronomy in combination with his work in geometry helped introduce the sundial in Greece. All of the information about Anaximander comes from a multitude of (sometimes conflicting) sources, but in all of them, it is established that he was one of the greatest thinkers of his time, and we now know that he laid the keystone for later Western philosophy.

Anaximenes Milesius, Philosophus, circa quinquagesimam quintam Olympiadem clarus habetur. Excessit e uiuis anno tertio sexagesimae nonae Olymp.

Anaximenes

Anaximenes of Miletus (6th century BCE), a pre-Socratic philosopher, was a disciple of Anaximander. Anaximenes was a member of the Milesian school of philosophy founded by Thales, although they disagreed on one key point. Thales believed that water was the fundamental element from which everything came. Anaximenes believed it was air, based on the belief that people were held together by souls composed of air. Thin out the air and you have fire, condense it and you have clouds, condense it further and you have water and earth.

With Anaximander, Anaximenes proposed that the Earth was a flattened disk floating on air at the centre of the Universe. The Sun moved around the Earth (but not underneath it) and was also a flat body made of fire. In this way, he differed with his predecessors like Thales, who held that water is the source of all things, and Anaximander, who thought that all things came from an unspecified boundless stuff.

1. Doctrine of Air

Anaximenes seems to have held that at one time everything was air. Air can be thought of as a kind of neutral stuff that is found everywhere and is available to participate in physical processes. Natural forces constantly act on the air, and transform it into other materials, which come together to form the organised world. In early Greek literature, air is associated with the soul (the breath of life), and Anaximenes may have thought of air as capable of directing its own development, as the soul controls the body. Accordingly, he ascribed to air divine attributes.

2. Doctrine of Change

Given his doctrine that all things are composed of air, Anaximenes suggested an interesting qualitative account of natural change:

"[Air] differs in essence in accordance with its rarity or density. When it is thinned, it becomes fire, while when it is condensed it becomes wind, then cloud, when still more condensed it becomes water, then earth, then stones. Everything else comes from these."

Using two contrary processes of rarefaction and condensation, Anaximenes explains how air is part of a series of changes. Fire turns to air, air to wind, wind to cloud, cloud to water, water to earth and earth to stone. Matter can travel this path by being condensed, or the reverse path from stones to fire by being successively more rarefied. Anaximenes provides a crude kind of empirical support by appealing to a simple experiment: if one blows on one's hand with the mouth relaxed, the air is hot; if one blows with pursed lips, the air is cold. Hence, according to Anaximenes we see that rarity is correlated with heat (as in fire), and density with coldness, (as in the denser stuff).

Anaximenes was the first recorded thinker who provided a theory of change and supported it with observation. Anaximander had described a sequence of changes that a portion of the boundless underwent to form the different stuffs of the world, but he gave no scientific reason for changes, nor did he describe any mechanism by which they might come about. By contrast, Anaximenes uses a process familiar from everyday experience to account for material change. He also seems to have referred to the process of felting, by which wool is compressed to make felt. This industrial process provides a model of how one stuff can take on new properties when it is compacted.

3. Origin of the Cosmos

Anaximenes, like Anaximander, gives an account of how our world came to be out of previously existing matter. According to Anaximenes, earth was formed from air by a felting process. It began as a flat disk. From evaporations from the earth, fiery bodies arose which came to be the heavenly bodies. The earth floats on a cushion of air. The heavenly bodies, or at least the sun and the moon, seem also to be flat bodies that float on streams of air. On one account, the heavens are like a felt cap that turns around the head. The stars may be fixed to this surface, like nails. In another account, the stars are like fiery leaves floating on air. The sun does not travel under the earth but circles around it and is hidden by the higher parts of the earth at night.

Like Anaximander, Anaximenes uses his principles to account for various natural phenomena. Lightning and thunder result from wind breaking out of clouds; rainbows are the result of the rays of the sun falling on clouds; earthquakes are caused by the cracking of the earth when it dries out after being moistened by rains. He gives an essentially correct account of hail as frozen rainwater.

Most commentators, following Aristotle, understand Anaximenes' theory of change as presupposing material monism. According to this theory, there is only one substance, (in this case air) from which all existing things are composed. The several things: wind, cloud, water, and so forth are only modifications of the real substance that is always and everywhere present. There is no independent evidence to support this interpretation, which seems to require Aristotle's metaphysical concepts of form and matter, substratum and accident that are too advanced for this period. Anaximenes may have supposed that the 'stuffs' simply change into one another in order.

4. Influence on Later Philosophy

Anaximenes' theory of successive change of matter by rarefaction and condensation was influential in later theories. It is developed by Heraclitus, and criticised by Parmenides. Anaximenes' general theory of how the materials of the world arise is adopted by Anaxagoras, even though the latter has a very different theory of matter. Both Melissus and Plato see Anaximenes' theory as providing a common-sense explanation of change. Diogenes of Apollonia makes air the basis of his explicitly monistic theory. The Hippocratic treatise "On Breaths" uses air as the central concept in a theory of diseases. By providing cosmological accounts with a theory of change, Anaximenes separated them from the realm of mere speculation and made them, at least in conception, scientific theories capable of testing.

Anaximander and Anaximenes: The Other Two Milesians

We talked about the history and evolution of philosophy as a discipline and the first natural philosopher known to us, Thales of Miletus. The next pre-Socratic natural philosopher we will be covering in this series is Anaximander, who was considered to be Thales' star student. He is thought to be the first philosopher who chose to write his thoughts and theories down. Whatever we have about Thales is due to the detailed accounts of his disciples and later on, Aristotle. Like Thales, Anaximander follows his belief that the world and nature are governed by discoverable laws instead of entirely being run on divine power and intervention.

Anaximander had his interests in geometry, astronomy, and with practical inventions. He was the first one to develop a cosmology, a philosophical view of the world. Much like Thales, a very small portion of his work survived. What we know of him comes from the accounts of different historical writers like, the 1st or 2nd century CE compiler of philosophical opinions Aëtius, the 3rd century theologian, antipope Hippolytus, and the 6th century Neoplatonist philosopher, Simplicius.

He is credited for making the first map of the known world, possibly based on previous travelers' notes. It was later corrected by his fellow Milesian, the author Hecataeus, a well-travelled man. He is also known to be the first one who introduced Greeks to the use of gnomon, which is somewhat of a sundial, and it demonstrated the equinoxes and solstices, and perhaps the hours of the day. He was also the first to think that the Earth was at the centre of the cosmos.

The shape of the Earth has always been a topic of great interest and even till now, there are groups who believe that the Earth is flat instead of the perceived and proven spherical shape of the planet. On the shape of Earth, Anaximander believed the inhabited land to be flat, like the top-flat shape of a cylinder, whose thickness is one-third of the diameter. He proposed that the planet is poised aloft, and it stays in its place as it is equidistant from all the things and hence is not in the disposition of 'flying off'. He also said that the Sun and the Moon were hollow rings of fire. Their disks are vents or holes in the rings, through which the fire can shine. The phases of the Moon as well as eclipses of the Sun and the Moon, are due to the vents' closing up.

Now, it is understandable that the entire theory sounds too out there, however, we can find some sense in the concepts by comparing them to the ones we have today. Anaximander thinking that the Sun and the Moon were filled with fire is far from what we know about them today but isn't very far from the concept that the Sun is a ball of fiery gas. Or his belief that living beings were evolutionary can also be considered an important theory. Since Man is a creature of nurture, he must have originated from some other organism because survival wouldn't have been possible as he was always in the state as he is now. It sounds like the foundational idea for the theory of evolution as we know it today.

While Anaximander and Thales agreed upon their natural and discoverable causes to the natural phenomenon theory, Anaximander did not agree with Thales' water theory (discussed in the last article). He came up with the idea of 'Apeiron' as a part of his cosmogony. He believed that all of the opposites that existed on the earth could not have appeared from a single element, which Thales identified to be water. He explained it to be a formless initial state. Apeiron literally means unlimited, boundless, indeterminate, and infinite. It lacks any limit or boundary, and it is undifferentiated. Apeiron wasn't an element, but it was primal formlessness. Unlike Thales who believed everything has originated from water, Anaximander believed that it came from the Apeiron. It is believed that he explained Apeiron as 'arche'.

Apeiron wasn't an element to Anaximander, and he made that glaringly clear. As stated in Aristotle's accounts, he used it to explain the opposite and destructive yet co-habitant nature of the elements of nature.

"Some have supposed... an unlimited something in addition to the elements, the matrix out of which they came. The reason for supposing this additional something, rather than air or water, for instance, to be unlimited, was that it seemed to evade the dilemma set out above. Since air is cold, water moist, and fire hot, and these properties are mutually destructive, an infinity of one of them would mean that the others would have perished this time, but this, they say, would not apply to an undifferentiated something out of which they all come."

The Apeiron is different from the other elements and becomes necessary if the primary elements are opposed. Such opposition is evident in the interrelation of these elements in the world. Anaximander characterises the relationships of these elements of the world as the one in continuous opposition. If either one of them overpowers the other, it would be completely destroyed. Hence, his arche is not one of the four elements but maybe intermediate between them.

He also postulated the concept of eternal motion along with the theory of Apeiron to explain the creation of the earth. This idea of eternal motion is what made it possible to separate the feelings/ sensations/ states of opposites from each other. It was responsible for the experience of opposite properties like hot/cold, dry/wet, heavy/light, etc. The idea of earth being in eternal motion sounds like the foundational idea to the contemporary phenomenon of Earth revolving around the Sun and rotating on its axis causing weather and days to change, respectively.

The world to Anaximander was not eternal and it was supposed to go where it all came from, the Apeiron, which would then form new worlds. Thus, all existing things must "pay penalty and retribution to one another for their injustice, according to the disposition of time," as he rather figuratively expressed it when he talks about 'cosmic justice'.

As I have already mentioned earlier, he was the first philosopher who had written his theories down to record them. He went ahead to create a unified account of nature and though his work was superseded very soon. He left an impact on the world with his questions and findings on the universe and its existence.

Moving on to our next philosopher, we come to Anaximenes, who was believed to be a student of the philosopher we just discussed above, Anaximander. All of the three Milesians were contemporaries. They were not successors. Their theories were not identical either, however, they were often built on top of others. We see a lot of similarities between the works of Anaximander and Anaximenes.

Much like Anaximander, Anaximenes recorded his theories as well. And like Anaximander, his works also haven't survived and can only be read about in the accounts of other philosophers who mentioned his work. His work didn't make it past the Hellenistic Age (age that starts after the death of Alexander the Great).

While looking for arche, a unifying principle of diversity, Thales went with his water theory while Anaximander went with Apeiron. Anaximenes went with 'aer' (ancient word for the element air). While his two predecessors came up with theories about what came from what, none of them was able to provide an explanation for the process of the change from one element to another. However, Anaximenes did, and it can be seen as his major contribution to the Milesian school of thought. He believed that land and rock arose from the water, and he explained this process through two processes of rarefaction and condensation.

"(Air) differs in essence in accordance with its rarity or density. When it is thinned it becomes fire, while it is condensed it becomes wind, then cloud, while still more condensed it becomes water, then earth, then stones. Everything else comes from these."

From the passage above, it becomes clear that he believed in degrees of condensation of moisture that corresponded to the densities of various types of matter. Air is common as it is the 'most evenly distributed', is invisible air of the atmosphere. By condensation, it becomes visible, first as mist or cloud, then like water, and finally as solid matter such as earth or stones. If further rarefied, it turns to fire. Thus, hotness and dryness typify rarity, whereas coldness and wetness are related to the denser matter. And part of this theory can be seen as a clear reflection of what we have today postulated as our water cycle, something that explains the basic and fundamental concept of rain through the methods of evaporation and condensation of water vapour (gas) to clouds which rain over the planet (liquid). It can be seen that Anaximenes was more or less correct when he explained how one element (water) changed into another.

However, a lot of people think of him as an ignorant, regressive and somewhat of a dumb philosopher. Here's why, when Thales understood his arche to be the element of water, Anaximander went on to systematically explain how the contrasting elements of nature could not have come from one single element, Anaximenes with his theory of air as the arche was regressive as instead of understanding or reasoning with Anaximander's theory of Apeiron. He simply went a step back to Thales and changed the material arche to air from water. However, there are significant similarities between Anaximenes' understanding of air as an arche and the concept of Apeiron. Anaximenes says that air is boundless and infinite, which is different from Thales' understanding of water and similar to that of the Apeiron. He also believed that the earth floated in the air in space which was in agreement with Anaximander's cosmology.

He didn't see air as we see and perceive it to be today. He drew his ideas from the ancient belief of air being the soul, breath of life. Aetius in his accounts writes about Anaximenes' idea of air.

"Just as our soul which is air holds us together, so breath and air surround the whole cosmos."

From the line, it becomes pretty obvious that he is talking about the air we breathe but he is also talking about much more than that. According to Cicero, Anaximenes said that air was God, it is boundless and infinite and always in motion.

Marcus Tullius Cicero was an orator, lawyer, politician, and philosopher born in 106 BCE. His life coincided with the decline and fall of the Roman Republic, and he was an important factor in many of the significant political events of his time. His writings are a valuable source of information to us about those events.

Elaborating this point further, his assumption that 'aer' is everlastingly in motion suggests that he thought it to possess life. Because it was eternally alive, 'aer' took on the qualities of the divine and became the cause of other gods as well as of all matter. He took the inspiration from metaphysics, as suggested by Anaximander while being in regression of Thales' ideas of the role of divinity, as explained in the previous article. The same motion accounts for the shift from one physical state of the 'aer' to another. There is evidence that he made the common analogy between the divine air that sustains the universe and the human "air", or soul, that animates people. Such a comparison between a macrocosm and a microcosm had also permitted him to maintain a unity behind diversity as well as to reinforce the view of his contemporaries that there is an overarching principle regulating all life and behavior.

The importance given to Anaximenes is conflicted but personally, he can be seen as the third step in a dialectic triad. In a dialectic triad, two positions contradict each other, the thesis and antithesis. Anaximenes, the third position, is the synthesis. He takes the good elements from both of his predecessors' theories and creates a new stance which resolves both into one. In the dialectic triad of the Milesian philosophers, Thales is the thesis who says that everything comes from a definable element, water. Anaximander is the antithesis who proposed that everything on the earth in the form of oppositional experiences couldn't have come from one single element and that everything is made from something undefinable and boundless, something that is immaterial. Anaximenes is the synthesis when he says that everything is made up from something definable, but boundless and material, but divine.

Xenophanes of Colophon was a travelling poet and philosopher who preceded Socrates by over a century. As is common with many pre-Socratic philosophers, there is little to go on when it comes to understanding Xenophanes. If he had written any extensive texts, they have not survived to this day. We instead must rely on a series of fragments attributed to the philosopher in order to understand his conception of God, which was controversial for the time.

What was it that Xenophanes proposed that was so revolutionary? Well, keep in mind that he lived in the times of classical Greece. The gods of Olympus were the accepted and venerated deities of the land. Zeus and his pantheon of gods weren't just characters in mythology; they were the central figures in a religion that would have been practised with a level of sincerity similar to that found among devout Christians today.

If you are familiar with any Greek mythology, you will know that the Olympians were not paradigms for virtue. Zeus was notoriously promiscuous, going so far as to transform into animals in order to carry out extramarital affairs with mortal women. Poseidon was wrathful, his anger prompting him to bat Odysseus back and forth across the seas for years after the hero blinded his Cyclops son, Polyphemus. The gods were known for, perhaps celebrated for, their imperfections, temper tantrums, proclivity for bloody vengeance and all around questionable behaviour. This understanding of the divine, however, is a grave injustice according to Xenophanes.

The wandering critic

We know more about Xenophanes's personality than we do about his biography. The fragments of Xenophanes's philosophy that remain suggest he was a strong character. He was deeply concerned with questions of morality. He disliked extravagance and overindulgence, although he admired those who could drink alcohol without losing their virtue (something Socrates later exemplified). He was preoccupied with the politics of his homeland of Colophon, and critical of the people of Colophon for their love of luxury, complaining that they went to the marketplace wearing extravagant clothes and "gorgeous long-flowing hair." And he was scornful of the religious thinking of his day.

Philosophy

Later philosophers didn't treat Xenophanes kindly; neither Plato nor Aristotle was particularly impressed by him. Nevertheless, what remains of his work suggests the keen and critical intelligence of a thinker with a wide range of interests. Xenophanes is still famous for his arguments about the nature of the gods and his criticism of anthropomorphism in religion.

POETRY

He is not worthy like me; for my poetic skill is better than

the strength of men or horses.

But this is quite randomly esteemed, and it is not right

to prefer strength to good poetic skill.

Thus, physical competition, as with the extreme physical ends and rivalry that can result from excessive drinking, are incompatible with the type of poetic skill and display that Xenophanes believes should be reserved for symposia. But I hasten to add that the denial of physical competition in no way implies a denial of intellectual competition, because, as we have seen, the symposium is an arena for the display of philosophical skill exemplified through competitive poetic performance. As others have argued, the archaic concept of σοφία 'skill' is discretely performative. It is not a latent ability but rather a summary of talents displayed through active and improvised performance. So what Xenophanes rejects at the physical level of athletic competition, he takes for granted in the intellectual atmosphere of the symposium.

For Xenophanes, the display of poetic expertise and the recalling and striving for virtue through poetic performance are meant to reinforce the distinctly ethical aims of the symposium. It is foremost in this respect that Xenophanes parts philosophical company with rhapsodes. Rhapsodes, Xenophanes implies, recite poetry without regard for its possible negative influence on the behaviour of the audience, while poetic performance in the symposium, by avoiding themes having to do with civil strife and warfare, is intended to edify and instruct its participants, indeed, to intensify social cohesion. Do Xenophanes protest too much?

On gods and horses

Xenophanes sets his sights on our tendency to anthropomorphise the gods. In a famous argument, Xenophanes points out that,

"But if horses or oxen or lions had hands or could draw with their hands and accomplish such works as men, horses would draw the figures of the gods as similar to horses, and the oxen as similar to oxen, and they would make the bodies of the sort which each of them had."

Not in our image? Not only does Xenophanes criticise our tendency to identify the gods with our worst traits, but — with keen insight — he also critiques the way that we make gods in our image. And this brings him to a claim about the gods that, in the context of his time, was remarkably novel.

"One god is greatest among gods and men, not at all like mortals in body or in thought."

Many have taken this as a claim for monotheism, and some later Christian readers have certainly read the passage like this. But the text itself is uncertain. Does Xenophanes mean that there is a god who has three attributes: being single ("one"), being great, and being unlike us? Or is he making the more modest claim that there is one particular god (among all the others) who has two attributes: they are the greatest, and they are unlike us?

Knowledge and true belief

In another tantalising fragment, Xenophanes appears to draw a distinction that becomes important to the later philosophical tradition: the distinction between true belief and knowledge. This is what he says:

"… and of course the clear and certain truth no man has seen nor will there be anyone who knows about the gods and what I say about all things. For even if, in the best case, one happened to speak just of what has been brought to pass, still he himself would not know. But opinion is allotted to all."

What Xenophanes seems to be saying is this: we all have opinions, and opinions come pretty cheap. If you give me a few seconds, I can probably come up with an opinion on anything at all. It might even happen that some of my opinions hit the mark. But even if they do hit the mark, this fortunate conjunction of my opinion with the reality of things does not add up to knowledge.

This caused some later philosophers, like the sceptic philosopher Sextus Empiricus, to claim that Xenophanes was arguing for the impossibility of true knowledge. Sextus may be overstating the case; but the distinction between opinion and "clear and certain truth" is a theme that recurs with the philosopher Parmenides, who takes up the challenge of distinguishing between the path of knowledge, and the path of mere opinion.

Legacy

Xenophanes travelled widely, reciting his poetry and, in so doing, spreading his beliefs. Among these was his recognition of the relativity and limitation of human understanding. He writes, "The gods have not revealed all things from the beginning to mortals but, by seeking, men find out, in time, what is better".

It is only by searching for the truth that one will find that truth. According to Xenophanes, one should not simply accept the beliefs of one's community as truth without questioning the validity of the concepts held.

Xenophanes' claim most certainly influenced later writers, most notably Socrates and, after him (as noted), Plato. Both of these later philosophers insisted on pursuing an individual course in pursuit of truth and wisdom. Xenophanes' concept of the one God, as noted above, influenced Parmenides' and the Eleatics' recognition of unity and their work contributed to Plato's Theory of Forms and Aristotle's Unmoved Mover, providing a philosophical basis for the development of monotheism.

Though quite different in specifics, Plato's Forms and Aristotle's Unmoved Mover both posit the existence of a 'higher' realm of reality which is responsible for the observable world. Xenophanes most likely would have approved of both these theories but, in keeping with his insistence on the small scope of human understanding, would have suggested both approached truth without being actually true. Xenophanes did not even consider his own views to be objectively true, only more valid than the beliefs of those around him.

Regarding his teaching, he writes, "Let these things, then, be taken as like the truth," not as truth itself. Only the one God knows the Truth, Xenophanes claimed, and mortals can only approach, never fully grasp, what that truth is. Different people and different cultures will interpret the Ultimate Truth differently, but these, in the end, are simply reflections of the Truth which is only known to itself.

A Greek philosopher of the late 6th century BCE, Heraclitus criticises his predecessors and contemporaries for their failure to see the unity in experience. He claims to announce an everlasting Word according to which all things are one, in some sense. Opposites are necessary for life but are unified in a system of balanced exchanges. The world itself consists of a law-like interchange of elements, symbolised by fire. Thus, the world is not to be identified with any particular substance, but rather with an ongoing process governed by a law of change. The underlying law of nature also manifests itself as a moral law for human beings. Heraclitus is the first Western philosopher to go beyond physical theory in search of metaphysical foundations and moral applications.

The Weeping Philosopher

Heraclitus became known in the centuries after his death as the 'weeping philosopher'. Why? As the ancient sources recorded, he spent many years alone, away from society. Also, he is attributed with a series of pessimistic (or rather elitist) statements in which he complained that the majority of people are unable to comprehend the Logos (cosmic reason). The 'weeping philosopher' became a commonplace title in the art of the subsequent centuries and Heraclitus often appeared crying next to a laughing Democritus, who was named the 'laughing philosopher' as his philosophy appeared more cheerful to later scholars. The most famous depiction of Heraclitus as a weeping philosopher is in Raphael's famous painting *The Academy of Athens*, where Raphael painted Michelangelo as Heraclitus sitting alone in the foreground of the image.

The Key Concepts of Heraclitus' Philosophy

Everything Is Fire?

During Heraclitus' time, Greek philosophers were trying to understand the universe, its true nature, and its underlying laws. Greek philosophers from the cities of Ionia were especially interested in uncovering what things are made of. These thinkers are also called monists because they claimed that everything in existence was made of a single element. First came Thales and said that everything was water. Then, Anaximenes stated that it was air. Anaximander proposed that an abstract substance called Apeiron was the basis of all things. Heraclitus took a stance on the matter. For him, the original and most basic element of all was fire.

"This world, which is the same for all, no one of gods or men has made; but it was ever, is now, and ever shall be an ever-living Fire, with measures of it kindling, and measures going out."

It can be also argued that he used fire as a vivid metaphor for change, which he understood to be the real basis of the universe. Just think of fire for a bit. It never stays the same, it never stays calm, it is always in movement. Heraclitus believed that this is the nature of everything. Everything constantly changes and takes the form of other things. The death of one thing is the birth of the other. In an endless circle, fire becomes air, air becomes water, and water becomes earth:

"Fire lives the death of air, and air lives the death of fire; water lives the death of earth, earth that of water."

The Unity of Opposites: The Birth of Dialectics

This idea of a world that is always moving and changing set the basis for what philosophers later called the dialectic; a method of philosophical inquiry whereby one finds a solution to a problem by examining two contradicting theses. So, why is Heraclitus the father of dialectics? Heraclitus believed that things tend to turn into their opposites given enough time. Life becomes death, day becomes night, and vice versa. If the night is going to turn into day how can we claim that they are opposites? In the grand scheme of things, day and night, just like all the other opposites, are more like the two sides of the same coin, just like yin and yang in Taoism. This idea is known as the unity of opposites. Let's take a look at some quotes by Heraclitus on the matter:

"The way up and the way down is one and the same."

"And it is the same thing in us that is quick and dead, awake and asleep, young and old; the former are shifted and become the latter, and the latter in turn are shifted and become the former."

The same applies to even mortals and immortals (heroes and gods):

"Mortals are immortals and immortals are mortals, the one living the others' death and dying the others' life."

Strife And War

But what truly makes Heraclitus the father of dialectics is his argument that harmony stems from the tension between opposite forces:

"There would be no harmony without high and low notes, and no animals without male and female, which are opposites."

"Men do not know how what is at variance agrees with itself. It is an attunement of opposite tensions, like that of the bow and the lyre."

The opposites are in constant strife with each other but also co-dependent. Without the one, the other cannot be:

"It is sickness that makes health pleasant; evil, good; hunger, plenty; weariness, rest."

In the Heraclitean universe, change does not occur on its own. There is a force that drives things forward, and that is strife. This is so important for Heraclitus, that he even rebukes Homer for wishing strife to disappear from the world! The Ephesian philosopher sees the strife between the opposites as essential, since the identity of one thing, depends on its strife with its opposite. This is so important that Heraclitus went as far as to even claim that:

"War is the father of all and the king of all; and some he has made gods and some men; some bond and some free."

Some scholars perceive this quote to be an endorsement of war. They argue that Heraclitus lived in an age of war and adopted a cynical stance that idealised conflict as the father of new empires and cultures. Others take this quote as a metaphor for the war between opposite forces in general.

Logos: The Concept that Inspired Philosophers

Logos is a term with multiple different meanings in Greek, including speech, argument, reason, proportion, discourse. For Heraclitus, Logos was the cosmic law that determines the way things take place. Heraclitus was the first in a great line of Greek philosophers to use Logos as a central part of his system in a way that favored abstraction, which is the reason why some later thinkers claimed that Heraclitus was the father of metaphysics. Logos was later used by Plato, Aristotle, the Stoics, the Neo-Platonists, and many more. Early Christian authors also loved using the Logos as a name for God.

The Relativism of Heraclitus

As Heraclitus believes in the unity of the opposites and the oneness of everything, he also reaches a point of relativism. Contrary to other Greek philosophers, Heraclitus claims that things depend on our point of view.

"The wisest man is an ape compared to God, just as the most beautiful ape is ugly compared to man."

"The sea is the purest and the impurest water. Fish can drink it, and it is good for them; to men it is undrinkable and destructive."

IDEAS THAT MAKE A DIFFERENCE

Heraclitus' philosophy is a good starting point for anyone concerned with change in life. Heraclitus said that life is like a river. The peaks and troughs, pits and swirls, are all are part of the ride. Do as Heraclitus would – go with the flow. Enjoy the ride, as wild as it may be.

Heraclitus was born into a wealthy family, but he renounced his fortune and went to live in the mountains. There, Heraclitus had plenty of opportunity to reflect on the natural world. He observed that nature is in a state of constant flux. "Cold things grow hot, the hot cools, the wet dries, the parched moistens," Heraclitus noted. Everything is constantly shifting, changing, and becoming something other than what it was before. Heraclitus concluded that nature is changing. Like a river, nature flows ever onwards. Even the nature of the flow changes. Heraclitus' vision of life is clear in his epigram on the river of flux:

"We both step and do not step in the same rivers. We are and are not."

One interpretation of this passage is that Heraclitus is saying we can't step into the same river twice. This is because the river is constantly changing. If I stroll down the banks of the Danube, the water before my eyes is not the same water from moment to moment. If the river is this water (which is a debatable point – the river could be its banks, the scar it carves in the landscape, but let's leave this aside), it follows that the Danube is not the same river from moment to moment. We step into the Danub and we step out of it again. When we step into it a second time, we step into different water and thus a different river.

Moreover, we step into and out of the river as different beings. Most interpretations of Heraclitus's river fragment focus on the idea of the river in a state of flux. But Heraclitus says more than this in this fragment: 'We are and are not'. The river changes, and so do we.

We are familiar with the principle of biological generation and corruption. Heraclitus puzzled over this principle two thousand years before the birth of the modern biological sciences and drew the ultimate lesson for the human condition. As material beings, we live in a world of flux. Moreover, we are flux. As physical bodies, we are growing and dying all the time, consuming light and resources to replicate our structure, while shedding matter continuously. Change and death are ubiquitous features of the natural world. Maybe this is what Heraclitus meant when he said, in his inimitable way:

"Gods are mortal, humans immortal, living their death, dying their life."

Parmenides is known as the founder of the Eleatic School of philosophy, which taught a strict Monistic view of reality. Philosophical Monism is the belief that all of the sensible world is of one basic substance and being that un-created and indestructible. According to the ancient writer Diogenes Laertius, Parmenides was a student of Xenophanes of Colophon - who some claim as the founder of the Eleatic School. Having mastered Xenophanes' teaching, Parmenides left to pursue his own vision. It is probable that he was Xenophanes' student, as the stamp of the elder philosopher's teachings can be seen in the work of Parmenides. Both assert that the things in life which one thinks one understands may be quite different than they seem to be, especially regarding an understanding of the gods.

Xenophanes' insistence on a single deity, who in no way resemble human beings, seems to have been the basis for Parmenides' claim of a single substance comprising all of reality. Parmenides was a younger contemporary of Heraclitus who claimed that all things are constantly in motion and that the First Cause - the basic "stuff" of life - is change itself. Parmenides' thought could not be further removed from that of Heraclitus in that Parmenides claimed nothing moves; change was an impossibility, and that human sense perception could not be relied upon for an apprehension of Truth.

The central vision of Parmenides' work is that change is an illusion - appearances change but not essence. This notion is later reflected in Plato's Theory of Forms, which claims that the observable world is only a reflection of a higher, truer reality.

Parmenides' Philosophy

Parmenides was probably a student of Xenophanes of Colophon, though this has been challenged just as the claim of Xenophanes as the founder of the Eleatic School was. It is probable, however, that Parmenides did study with Xenophanes because Xenophanes vision of a single, all-powerful god, unlike human beings or human conceptions of deities, as well as the other fragments of his work arguing for a higher realm of understanding which is misinterpreted by human beings, is similar in many ways to Parmenides' vision.

Xenophanes claimed that people were mistaken about the nature of the gods and, so, the nature of the world. Parmenides said the same, writing:

"There is a way which is and a way which is not [a way of truth and a way of opinion]. There is not, nor will there be, anything other than what is since indeed Destiny has fettered it to remain whole and immovable. Therefore those things which mortals have established, believing them to be true, will be mere names: 'coming into being and passing away,' 'being and not being,' 'change of place'."

Parmenides argues here that one may think the world one lives in is composed of multiples, but, in reality, it is One and unchanging. Reality, he insisted, had to be One because all things received their being and substance from it. The dog and horse, though they may appear different animals, participated in the form and function of living things, just as human beings did, and so, in essence, all three were the same. Nothing, he claimed, is capable of inherently changing in any significant fashion because the very substance of reality is immutable.

A contemporary of both Heraclitus and Socrates, Parmenides's beliefs would contradict the former and influence the latter. Heraclitus based his philosophy on the concept of fire as the First Cause of existence and change as synonymous with life itself. Life, to Heraclitus, was changed in that it was continually in motion, nothing was permanent, and one person or experience continually gave way to others. Parmenides rejected Heraclitus' argument as informed by the senses and so mistaken.

Parmenides' insistence on one ultimate Truth would significantly affect Socrates' young student Plato, who developed Parmenides' monism through his own Theory of Forms. Plato paid homage to the older philosopher by devoting three of his dialogues to Eleatic though: the *Parmenides*, the *Statesman*, and the *Sophist*. In the *Parmenides*,

Parmenides and his student Zeno of Elea come to Athens and instruct a young Socrates in wisdom and this, perhaps, is Plato's most direct acknowledgement of his debt to Parmenides' thought.

Parmenides Founded the School of Elea

Parmenides founded the philosophical school of Elea, and his most important pupil was Zeno, who was also widely understood to be his lover. Parmenides' philosophical influences are obscure. One concrete forerunner of Parmenides was Xenophanes, who is known for distinguishing different forms of knowledge and belief (among other achievements). His only surviving written work is a poem allegedly titled *The House of Night and Day*.

Parmenides' poem recounts what Parmenides learned from the Goddess who lives in the house of night and day. It begins with the description of his visit to the Goddess' house.

"O young man, accompanied by immortal charioteers / and mares who bear you as you arrive at our abode, / welcome, since a fate by no means ill sent you ahead to travel / this way (for surely it is far from the track of humans), / but Right and Justice."

The opening of Parmenides' poem is noteworthy for a number of reasons. The reference to "a fate by no means ill" is often understood as a reference to various other mythical accounts of the House of Night and Day, most famously that of Hesiod, which present it as a place of judgement for the souls of the dead.

The "House of Night and Day" Is a Metaphor

The notion that the place where the dead come for judgement serves as the home of the Goddess who will enlighten Parmenides can only be understood as a claim for the eternal and unchanging veracity of his philosophy. The fact that he is described as a young man similarly suggests that Parmenides is putting distance between himself and the pre-philosophical wise men. The kind of knowledge he seeks is not the result of the aggregation of experience. The poem continues in a way which sharpens this implication,

"You must needs learn all things, / both the unshaken heart of well-rounded reality/ and the notions of mortals, in which there is no genuine trustworthiness. / Nonetheless these things too will you learn, how what they resolved."

The Ways of Inquiry Point Towards an Obvious and an Unobvious Reality

One way of understanding the contrast between the different ways of inquiry is as an attempt to distinguish the fluid presuppositions of everyday life from the reality as it is unchangingly. That is, it constitutes an argument not in favour of any particular metaphysics – to use a prominent recent definition from Adrian Moore, the most general possible attempt to make sense of things – but something which foreruns that, namely an attempt to define that attempt apart from the logic of everyday life and the assumptions of ordinary people. This is a kind of aristocratic, urbane impulse which one can recognize in many Greek thinkers, and the view that real knowledge is unobvious, subtle and distant from the assumptions which most people precede from is one of the most persisting features of Western philosophy.

Nothing Can Come from Nothing

It seems that Parmenides' claims were hard to comprehend for his listeners, necessitating Zeno's mathematical paradoxes. Parmenides' main point was simply that nothing could come from nothing. He argued that being must have always existed, and that reality was uniform, unbroken, and unbreakable. He writes:

"There is left but this single path to tell thee of: namely, that being is. And on this path, there are many proofs that being is without beginning and indestructible; it is universal, existing alone, immovable and without end; nor ever was it nor will it be, since it now is, all together, one, and continuous. For what generating of it wilt thou seek out? From what did it grow, and how? I will not permit thee to say or to think that it came from not-being; for it is impossible to think or to say that not-being is. What would then have stirred it into activity that should arise from not-being later rather than earlier? So, it is necessary that being either is absolutely or is not. Nor will the force of the argument permit that anything springs from being except being itself. Therefore, justice does not slacken her fetters to permit generation or destruction but holds being firm."

Being & Not Being

Simply put, his argument is that since 'something' cannot come from 'nothing' then 'something' must have always existed in order to produce the sensible world. This world one perceives, then, is of one substance - that same substance from which it came. Those who inhabit it share in this same unity of substance. Therefore, if it should appear that a person is born from 'nowhere' or that one dies and goes somewhere else, both perceptions must be wrong since that which is now can never have been 'not' nor can it ever 'not be'.

In this, Parmenides may be developing ideas from the earlier philosopher Pythagoras, who claimed the soul is immortal and returns to the sensible world repeatedly through reincarnation. If so, however, Parmenides radically departed from Pythagorean thought which not only allows for, but depends upon, plurality. Change is not only possible in life, to Pythagoras, but necessary in order for life to be life. To Parmenides, and his disciples of the Eleatic School (including, possibly, Melissus of Samos), such a claim would be evidence of belief in the senses which, they insisted, could never be trusted to reveal the truth.

Conclusion

The single path of truth which Sophia calls Parmenides to pursue is the path of unity and recognition of the underlying interconnectedness of all things. Toward the end of the poem, when he writes how "men have determined in their minds to name two principles" and, in doing so, have gone wrong. He highlights what he sees as the essential problem people have in perceiving reality: the belief in plurality.

As long as one sees one's self as distinct from everyone else, and each other person as their own entity, and the earth beneath one's feet as separate from one's self and others, and animals still more different than earth or people, one will be inclined to treat all things outside of one's self as separate, foreign, leaving the individual alone to navigate the world. Understanding the essential Oneness of reality - how all people and animals and the earth and sky are of the same basic substance and connected on the deepest level - encourages full participation of everyone in life because every seeming individual was not a lone entity but part of everything else.

Zeno of Elea, a pre-Socratic Greek philosopher, flourished about 450 BCE. Elea was a Greek colony in southern Italy, on the west coast, below modern Naples, not too far from where the Pythagoreans had set up their own colony, in Croton. Elea emerged on the map of pre-Socratic philosophy when Parmenides of Elea, around 475, wrote a book with the title *On Nature*. In it, Parmenides argued that change is an illusion; that there is only one thing in the world, Being, and Being, logically, cannot change. That created quite a problem for natural philosophers, such as Heraclitus of Ephesus, who focused their attention on the nature of change. We wrote a post on Parmenides several months ago, and one on Heraclitus before that.

Zeno was a junior disciple of Parmenides, part of what is called the Eleatic School. He took it upon himself to provide further evidence for the illusory nature of change, by proposing a series of paradoxes, now known as Zeno's Paradoxes. There seem to have been nine of them; four of which were discussed in detail by later writers such as Plato and Aristotle. We will present just two of them here, which will be enough for you to get the idea.

Achilles and the Tortoise

The most famous Paradox of Zeno is Achilles and the Tortoise. Consider that Achilles is going to race a tortoise. The tortoise, reasonably, has been given a head start. One can break the race down into stages, says Zeno. In the first stage, Achilles runs up to where the tortoise was at the start of the race, say point A. But the tortoise will, in the meantime, have advanced a little, to point B. In the second stage, Achilles races to point B. Meanwhile, the tortoise advances a little further to point C. In the third stage, Achilles runs to point C, and the Tortoise ambles to point D. And so it goes. Zeno has broken the race down into an infinite number of stages, and Achilles could never go through infinite segments in a finite time. Ergo, Achilles cannot catch the tortoise. The fact that, if we staged such a race, we could observe Achilles passing the tortoise in very little time, just deepens the paradox.

The Dichotomy Paradox

A second paradox, which is even more confounding, is sometimes called the Dichotomy Paradox, which is puffery – it should just be called the Stay-at-Home Paradox. Here Zeno points out that if you want to run from point A to point B, you first must reach a halfway point, C. But before you can get to C, you must arrive at point D, which is halfway to C. And before you get to D, you will have to reach point E, halfway to D. And so it goes, ad infinitum. You can, in fact, never leave A, or so the paradox demonstrates.

Multiplicity and Oneness

First, Socrates offers a succinct interpretation of Zeno of Elea's negation of multiplicity in general: "If the things that are, are many, then they must be both like and unlike, but this is impossible. For neither can unlike things be like, nor like things unlike? Is this not what you say?"

We can think of the negation of multiplicity in this context as the denial of the existence of many things and of things with many qualities. The critical philosophical move of Parmenidean philosophy, of which Zeno appears to have been a staunch advocate, amounts to the belief that some of these qualities are mutually exclusive. They cannot be held at the same time, or are perhaps directly contradictory. What follows from this, on Socrates' reading of Zeno, is simply that "contrary to everything normally said, that there are not many things." This belief in the "oneness" of things we can call Monism.

Paradox and Monism

The belief that there is, in a strict sense, only one thing is just one interpretation of various common interpretations Parmenides, and therefore we can understand Zeno of Elea's commitment to oneness in a plethora of ways. Accepting that proviso, however, we should also emphasise that this is a self-consciously unintuitive philosophy. Zeno here explicitly accepts that it runs against common sense.

The relationship between philosophical theory, and the assumptions by which we lead our daily lives is a major concern for philosophers of almost every period. This tension can also be understood to relate Zeno's Parmenidean Monism to his paradoxes, because these paradoxes attempt to show that several common-sense assumptions, which we are equally unwilling to relinquish are, in fact, contradictory.

Having already noted that Zeno appears to acknowledge that his philosophy at large is not intuitive, these paradoxes are not simply puzzles, but puzzles with a point: namely, the incoherence and problematization of common sense in philosophy. This purpose was at least as central to Zeno's development of paradoxes as was his determination to defend a negation of multiplicity directly.

The First Paradox: Limited and Unlimited Things

The closest thing we have to a fragment of Zeno of Elea's philosophical work comes from Simplicius, a Neoplatonist and commentator on Aristotle. He quoted Zeno: "If there are many things, it is necessary that they be just as many as they are and neither greater than themselves nor fewer. But if they are just as many as they are, they will be limited. If there are many things, the things that are are unlimited; for there are always others between these entities, and again others between those. And thus, the things that are, are unlimited."

In effect, this paradox holds that if there are many things, there are finitely many things and if there are many things, there are infinitely many things. The critical move here is the movement from posting multiplicity – that is, the existence of many things – to positing the existence of an unlimited number of intermediate things, states, qualities and so forth.

The Second Paradox: A Paradox of Motion

This is also the central thought behind one of Zeno's most famous paradoxes, and it comes to us from Aristotle: "First, there is the argument about its being impossible to move because what moves must reach the half-way point earlier than the end... Therefore, the argument of Zeno falsely presumes that it is not possible to traverse or make contact with unlimited things individually in a limited time."

The basic idea here is simple to grasp, and extremely powerful. If we imagine ourselves moving from Point A to Point B, we must also imagine ourselves moving from Point A to a point between Point A and Point B. If we call that middle point Point C, then in order to get to that point we must first move past a middle point between Point A and Point C. This can continue ad infinitum, and the problem this creates for us is that there seem to be infinitely many intermediate points between any two given points, which seems to suggest that there are infinitely many different points that exist between any two given points.

How can we expect to move through infinitely many points in a limited period of time? This seems impossible, and yet we do, in fact, move.

The Reasoning Behind the Paradoxes: Zeno and Infinity

We are again forced to confront Zeno of Elea's conception of intermediacy as a dimension of his paradoxes and his wider thought. Zeno seems convinced that between two different things, there must be other, intermediate things. This is the central thought behind both of the paradoxes we have examined so far, and because it isn't obvious why it would be so, we need to clarify what motivates it.

John Palmer offers the following, succinct explanation: "Any two things will be distinct or separate from one another only if there is some other thing between them. Two representative things, $x1$ and $x2$, will be distinct only if there is some other thing, $x3$, between them. In turn, $x1$ and $x3$ will be distinct only if there is some other thing, $x4$, between them. Since the postulate can be repeatedly applied in this manner unlimited times, between any two distinct things there will be limitlessly many other things. Therefore, if there are many things, then there must be limitlessly many things."

Reception and Responses to Zeno of Elea's Paradoxes

There isn't space to cover all of Zeno's paradoxes here, but it is worth saying something about how they have been received since. As mentioned previously, the argumentative force of the paradoxes seems to be greatly dependent on their problematization of everyday assumptions. That is especially true for our assumptions about physical bodies.

It isn't hard to see why Zeno is often credited as the inventor not just of the paradox, but of the reductio ad absurdum; to take an argument to its natural conclusion, and by carrying the thought which lies behind an assumption beyond the environment in which that assumption developed, and therefore the environment in which it makes sense, demonstrate the contingency of such an assumption.

Arguably, the development of physical theories which run against the assumptions we ordinarily make about the external world is the first step towards the development of natural science in the Greek world, and therefore modern science as it is practiced today.

Plato's Criticism

Among those who were critical of Zeno's paradoxes was Plato. Plato's philosophy was significantly influenced by Parmenides in the development of his Theory of Forms, a higher realm of Truth of which the observable world was only a reflection. Like Parmenides' unchanging essence, Plato's Forms were perfect, eternal, and informed the world of the senses which was largely illusory. At the same time, however, Plato criticized Zeno's paradoxes as establishing confusing paradigms and missing the fundamental truth of Oneness.

In his dialogue of the *Parmenides*, Plato sets down the fundamental criticism of the claims of Parmenides and Zeno when he has Socrates say:

"If a person could prove the absolute like to become unlike, or the absolute unlike to become like, that, in my opinion, would indeed be a wonder; but there is nothing extraordinary, Zeno, in showing that the things which only partake of likeness and unlikeness experience both. Nor, again, if a person were to show that all is one by partaking of one, and at the same time many by partaking of many, would that be very astonishing. But if he were to show me that the absolute one was many, or the absolute many one, I would be truly amazed. And so, of all the rest: I should be surprised to hear that the natures or ideas themselves had these opposite qualities; but not if a person wanted to prove to me that I was many and also one. When he wanted to show that I was many he would say that I have a right and a left side, and a front and a back, and an upper and a lower half, for I cannot deny that I partake of multitude; when, on the other hand, he wants to prove that I am one, he will say, that we who are here assembled are seven, and that I am one and partake of the one. In both instances he proves his case.

So again, if a person shows that such things as wood, stones, and the like, being many are also one, we admit that he shows the coexistence the one and many, but he does not show that the many are one or the one many; he is uttering not a paradox but a truism. If however, as I just now suggested, someone were to abstract simple notions of like, unlike, one, many, rest, motion, and similar ideas, and then to show that these admit of admixture and separation in themselves, I would be very much astonished. This part of the argument appears to be treated by you, Zeno, in a very spirited manner; but, as I was saying, I should be far more amazed if anyone found in the ideas themselves which are apprehended by reason, the same puzzle and entanglement which you have shown to exist in visible objects."

In this passage, Socrates is asking how the 'many' can be 'one' in the physical, not just the abstract, world. The board, hammer, and nail placed on the table are, clearly, three objects which do not partake in the properties of each other. The board is made of wood, the hammer of wood and metal, the nail of metal alone. These objects cannot possibly be categorized as 'one' but must, of necessity, be considered 'many'. Since, according to Socrates' argument here, Zeno never moves beyond observable phenomena to make his point, the truth of the uniformity of reality remains unproven.

Zeno's Response

Zeno countered this argument by showing that the 'many' have to be 'one' because, for plurality to exist, logic could not. Since logical sequence and understanding does exist, there can be no plurality. Professor J. M. Robinson comments on this,

"As we can see from the first hypothesis of the first argument of Zeno's treatise, the thesis that things are a many give rise to consequences that are inconsistent even with one another; for if things are a many they must be 'both like and unlike' and this is impossible not because it violates sense perception, but because it violates the law of contradiction, which lies at the basis of all thought. "

One cannot, then, claim that the board, hammer, and nail are 'many' in that the three objects partake of the same basic substance of the One. A person may look at the three objects and claim there are 'many' objects on the table but that would only be an expression of trust in sense perception, not a valid apprehension of the truth. Further, the claim that there is a "many" which constitutes reality, instead of a One, makes logic impossible because one would then be dealing with the many realities of each individual person but, because logical discourse and philosophical argument is possible. Therefore, there must be some common ground shared by all — this common ground is Being.

Conclusion

Zeno maintained that trust in the senses leads to contradictory conclusions, in that something which exists and 'is' cannot not exist and not be, and yet one's senses tell one that everything is always changing from what it 'is' to something it 'is not'. Sense perception supports the claim of the Pre-Socratic philosopher Heraclitus - with whom both Parmenides and Zeno disagreed - that "Life is Flux" and everything is in constant motion and transformation. To Heraclitus, the First Cause was fire - a transformative element - and this reflected the actual nature of life which was, in fact, constant change itself.

To Zeno, this was a faulty conclusion based upon unreliable sense perception. That which cannot not be because it would then contain within itself the contradiction of having the qualities of 'being' and 'not being' and, as this defies logic, it cannot be held as true. In this, both Parmenides and Zeno were at complete odds with the philosophy of Heraclitus but, at the same time, seemed to share his belief that the majority of human beings could not, or would not, seek to understand the truth behind the apparent reality which the senses provide. Although all three philosophers argued against acceptance of sense perception as truth, they acknowledged that people in general are more comfortable with calling their perceptions and opinions "truth" than questioning them.

That concession to each other would be as far as they would go, however, in that the philosophical vision of Heraclitus was completely opposed to the Monist view. Parmenides' Monism and Zeno's paradoxes could admit no truth of plurality and remain cohesive. In their view, they did not have to because one could admit to the appearance of change without acknowledging any kind of change in the essence of fundamental reality.

Empedocles was a philosopher and poet: one of the most important philosophers working before Socrates, and a poet of outstanding ability and of great influence upon later poets such as Lucretius. His works, *On Nature and Purifications*, exist in more than 150 fragments. He has been regarded variously as a materialist physicist, a shamanic magician, a mystical theologian, a healer, a democratic politician, a living god, and a fraud. To him is attributed the invention of the four-element theory of matter, one of the earliest theories of particle physics, put forward seemingly to rescue the phenomenal world from the static monism of Parmenides. Empedocles' worldview is of a cosmic cycle of eternal change, growth and decay, in which two personified cosmic forces, Love and Strife, engage in an eternal battle for supremacy.

In psychology and ethics, Empedocles was a follower of Pythagoras. Hence, he was a believer in the transmigration of souls, and also a vegetarian. He claims to be a daimon —a divine or potentially divine being — banished from the immortals gods for "three times countless years" for committing the sin of meat-eating and forced to suffer successive reincarnations in an purificatory journey through the different orders of nature and elements of the cosmos, and he has now achieved the most perfect of human states and will be reborn as an immortal. He also claimed seemingly magical powers, including the ability to revive the dead and to control the winds and rains.

Physics

The foundations of Empedocles' physics lie in the assumption that there are four 'elements' of matter, or 'roots' as he calls them, using a botanical metaphor that stresses their creative potential: earth, air, fire and water. These are able to create all things, including all living creatures, by being 'mixed' in different combinations and proportions. Each of the elements, however, retains its own characteristics in the mixture, and each is eternal and unchanging. The positing of these four roots of matter forms part of a tradition of opposite material creative principles in Presocratic philosophy, but it also has its origins in an attempt to counter the theories of Parmenides who had argued that the world is single and unchanging since nothing can come from nothing and nothing can be destroyed into nothing — a theory known as Eleatic monism.

Empedocles' response was to appropriate Parmenides' ideas and to use them against themselves. Nothing can come from nothing nor be destroyed into nothing, and therefore, in order to rescue the reality of the phenomenal world, there must be something eternal and unchanging beneath the constant change, growth, and decay of the visible world. Empedocles then transfers the changelessness that Parmenides attributes to the entire world to his four elements and replaces the static singularity Parmenides' world with a dynamic plurality. The four elements correspond closely to their expression at the macroscopic level of nature, with the traditional quadripartite division of the cosmos into earth, sea, air, and the fiery aether of the heavenly bodies. This division at the macroscopic level of reality is applied reductively at the microscopic level to produce a parallelism between the constituents of matter and the fundamental constituents of the cosmos, but the reduction of the world into four types of material particles does not deny the reality of the world we see, but instead validates it. Empedocles stresses this parallel between the elements at the different levels of reality by using the terms 'sun', 'sea', and 'Earth' interchangeably with 'fire', 'water', and 'earth'. Of the four elements, although Empedocles stresses their equality of powers, fire is also granted a special role both in its hardening effect on mixtures of the other elements and also as the fundamental principle of living things.

Cosmology

Empedocles also posits two cosmic forces which work upon the elements in both creative and destructive ways. These he personifies as Love – a force of attraction and combination – and Strife – a force of repulsion and separation. Whether these cosmic forces are to be envisaged in simply mechanistic terms as descriptions of the way things happen, or as expressions of internal properties of the elements, or as external forces that act upon the elements, is not clear. It is also unclear whether the two forces are to be seen as impersonal mechanistic physical forces or as intelligent divinities that act in purposive ways in creation and destruction. Evidence can be found for all these interpretations. What is clear is that these two forces are engaged in an eternal battle for domination of the cosmos and that they each prevail in turn in an endless cosmic cycle. The details of this cosmic cycle are also difficult to establish, but the most widely accepted interpretation is represented in the following diagram:

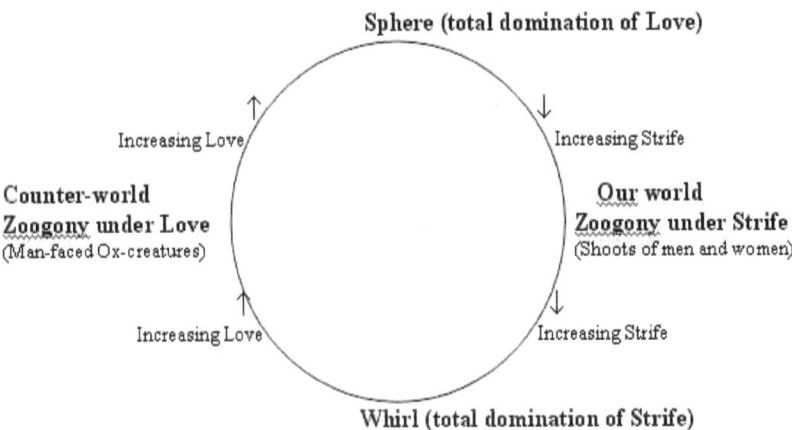

Empedocles' Cosmic Cycle

Beginning from the top of the diagram and proceeding clockwise, when Love is completely dominant, she draws all the elements fully together into a Sphere in which, although the elements are not fused together into a single mass, each is indistinguishable from the others. The Sphere then, is an a-cosmic state during which no matter can exist, and no life is possible. Then as Love's power gradually weakens and Strife begins to grow in power, he gradually separates out the elements from the Sphere until there is enough separation for matter to come into existence, for the world to be created and for all life to be born. When Strife has achieved total domination, we again get an a-cosmic state in which the elements are separated completely, and the world and all life is destroyed in a Whirl. Then Love begins to increase in power and to draw the elements together again, and as she does so the world is again created, and life is again born. When Love has achieved full dominance we return once more to the sphere.

"A twofold tale I shall tell: at one time it grew to be one only from many, and at another again it divided to be many from one. There is a double birth of what is mortal, and a double passing away; for the uniting of all things brings one generation into being and destroys it, and the other is reared and scattered as they are again being divided. And these things never cease their continuous exchange of position, at one time all coming together into one through Love, at another again being borne away from each other by Strife's repulsion."

The cosmos exists in a state of constant flux then, beneath which there is a certain sort of stability in the eternity of the elements. The world is in a constant state of organic evolution, and there appear to be two different creations and two different worlds which have no direct link between them. According to the most widely accepted interpretation Empedocles considered that we ourselves inhabit the world under the increasing power of Strife.

Biology

Empedocles' physics have a particularly biological focus, as is indicated by his choice of the botanical metaphor of 'roots' for what were later called 'elements'. The term 'roots' stresses the creative potential of the roots rather than illustrating the way they create things by being mixed in different combinations. 'Elements' is the word for the letters of the alphabet, and is a metaphor that stresses the ability of the elements of matter to form different types of matter by interchange of position just as a limited number of letters are able to form all sorts of different words on the page. To illustrate this aspect of the creative abilities of his roots, Empedocles uses an analogy with the way painters can use a limited number of colours to create all sorts of different colours and represent all the different productions of nature.

"As painters, men well taught by wisdom in the practice of their art, decorate temple offerings when they take in their hands pigments of various colours, and after fitting them in close combination – more of some and less of others – they produce from them shapes resembling all things, creating trees and men and women, animals and birds and water-nourished fish, and long-lived gods too, highest in honour; so let not error convince you in your mind that there is any other source for the countless perishables that are seen, but know this clearly, since the account you have heard is divinely revealed."

Among other aspects, this analogy exhibits Empedocles' tendency to think about the creative abilities of the elements in terms of their biological products, here a characteristically Empedoclean list of creatures representing the different orders of nature: plants, humans, land animals, birds, and fish, as well as gods. If painters use a mixture of a small number of pigments to produce copies of the works of nature, then the same process is productive of those works of nature. In other ways as well in his presentation of the cosmic cycle and the endless combination and separation of the elements he tends to elide the distinction between the elements and the life-forms they produce. Just as in the parallel he draws between the elements of the cosmos on both microscopic and macroscopic levels, so a close parallel is drawn between living creatures and their constituent elements.

a. Origin of Species

Empedocles presents us with the earliest extant attempt at producing a detailed rational mechanism for the origin of species. Greek traditions include the aetiological myths of the origin of a particular species of animal by transformation from a human being. The origins of humans, or of particular heroes, founders of cities or of races is frequently explained by what I term a botanical analogy. They originally emerged autochthonously from the ground just as plants do today, and this is also standard in ancient scientific theories as well. The original spontaneous generation of life from the earth, with all creatures emerging in their present species. Empedocles attempts to provide a comprehensive mechanism for the origins not simply of humans or of a particular animal but of all animal life, including humans, and a rational mechanism that would seem to do away with the need for any design in creatures or any external agency to order them and separate them into their individual species.

We now find the following lines in which Empedocles seemingly introduces his account of zoogony:

"I will show you to your eyes too, where they find a larger body: first the coming together and the unfolding of birth, and as many as are now remaining of this generation. This is to be seen among the wilder species of mountain-roaming beasts; this is to be seen in the twofold offspring of men, this is to be seen in the produce of the root-bearing fields and of the cluster of grapes mounting on the vine. From these convey to your mind unerring proofs of my account: for you will see the coming together and unfolding of birth."

Empedocles promises an exposition of zoogony. The origin of species which, from the examples he gives – wild animals, humans and plants – is clearly intended to encompass all animal and plant life, including humans. He appeals to present day species as proof of his theories: we can see both the products of this process of zoogony around us in nature today and also, it seems, we can see the same processes still going on today. That the theory refers to present day species rather than creatures in some counter world is underlined by the stress Empedocles puts on 'as many as are now remaining of this generation'. So, the theory is intended to explain the origin and development of all life and refers specifically to the animals and plants around us today, both as examples of and as proofs of the theory he will propose. This process of generation he describes by the repeated 'the coming together and the unfolding of birth'. This seems to posit two processes which work, either together or separately, to produce the life we see around us today. A process of coming together and also a process of unfolding or perhaps more strictly 'unleafing' since the metaphor originates from the leaves of plants. So, the second part of this process of zoogony involves a botanical metaphor: just as in the traditional botanical analogy of the myths of autochthony, an appeal to the development and growth of plants is used to describe the process of the development of all life.

First of all, individual limbs and organs were produced from the earth. These wandered separately at first, and then, under the combining power of Love, they came together in all sorts of wild and seemingly random hybrid combinations, producing double fronted creatures, hermaphrodites, ox-faced man creatures and man-faced ox-creatures. This weird picture is explained by Aristotle in the *Physics* and later in more detail by Simplicius in his commentary on the *Physics* as a theory of the origin of species in which, as we would put it, a certain form of natural selection is operative. The creatures assembled wrongly from parts of disparate animals will die out, either immediately, or by being unable to breed, and only the creatures by chance put together from homogeneous limbs will survive and so go on to find the species that we see today. The production of species and their ordering then is explained by a mechanistic process long recognised as a forerunner of Darwin's theory of natural selection. Unlike in Darwin's theory however, there would seem to be no gradual evolution of one species into another, and all of the variety of nature is produced in a great burst of birth in the beginning and is then whittled down by extinctions into the creatures we see today. That this theory intends to account for the origins of both humans and animals is ensured by the component parts of the ox-headed man-creatures and man-headed ox-creatures. There will clearly also be created by this system man-headed man-creatures and ox-headed ox-creatures, that is to say normal oxen and normal humans, although they are not mentioned. Further evidence that this zoogony relates to present day creatures is given by Aristotle and Simplicius who tell us that this process is still going on today.

Empedocles also adds to this theory another explanation of the origins of humans very much along the lines of traditional myths of autochthony. Strasbourg describes the 'shoots' of men and women arising from the earth, drawn up by fire as it separates out from the other elements during the creation under the power of increasing Strife. As his choice of the word 'shoots' indicates these are not yet fully articulated people with distinct limbs but 'whole-nature forms' that 'did not as yet show the lovely shape of limbs, or voice or language native to man'. We may assume that as Strife increases in power these 'shoots' will, just as plant buds do, gradually become fully articulated with distinct limbs and features. So human origins are accounted for by a botanical analogy, with humans as biological productions of the earth itself. This theory is also intended to account for modern-day as humans, as Strasbourg fr. d tells us 'Even now daylight beholds their remains'. So, both the creation under Love and the creation under Strife refer to the origins of modern plants, animals, and humans. This is problematic since according to the picture of the cosmic cycle given above the world created by Strife is quite separate from that created by Love, and two quite different explanations are given by Empedocles for each creation of life. Various attempts have been made to account for this, including a radical revision of the cosmic cycle in order to allow both creations of life to take place within the same world, and also seeing the two different worlds of the cosmic cycle as more useful devices for examining different aspects of creation separately than absolutely chronologically separate phases of a cycle: the work of Love in combining creatures and the work of Strife in articulating them would then actually take place at the same time, but are simply described as operative in chronologically separate phases.

Embryology

Empedocles is an exponent of the pangenetic theory of embryology. In this theory, inheritance of characteristics from both mother and father is explained by each of the two parents' limbs and organs creating tiny copies of themselves. These miniature limbs and organs then flow together in the generative seed and when the two seeds combine in the womb the father's seed may provide the model for the nose, while the mother's seed the model for the eyes and so on. This is an elegant way of accounting for inheritance of characteristics, but this is unlikely to be the whole story. As Aristotle points out there are strong conceptual similarities between Empedocles' embryology and the creation under Love in which we see the coming together of pre-formed limbs creating life. So, Empedocles thinks of the original formation of animals as a process analogous to the present-day formation of the embryo in the womb. From his description in Strasbourg, 'the coming together and unfolding of birth' we seem to have two processes that are at work in the formation of both present day creatures and the original creation of life. The 'coming together' describes both the original coming together of the limbs of the first creatures and also the coming together of the tiny limbs in conception. The other side of the creative process, the 'unfolding' is illustrated by the creation under Strife of the 'shoots of men and pitiable women' whose limbs are at first not fully articulated or defined: they will undergo a process of 'unfolding' just like plant buds and become fully developed humans. This 'unfolding' is clearly paralleled in embryology by the gradual development and growth of the embryo in the womb. Therefore, it may be best to think of the tiny limbs and organs contained in the generative seed not as fully developed limbs and organs, but as the genetic material that contains the potential for the development of limbs and organs. This is somewhat speculative, but would provide Empedocles with a much more nearly truly evolutionary theory of the origin of species than had previously been ascribed to him. Certainly the differentiation into the two sexes is described in terms of potential: the warmth of the womb determines whether the embryo will be male or female, 'They were poured in pure places; some met with cold and became women', 'For the male was warmer... this is the reason why men are dark, more powerfully built, and hairier'. It may be that other characteristics are also determined or informed by environmental factors as well.

c. Perception and Thought

Empedocles seems to have been the first philosopher to give a detailed explanation of the mechanism by which we perceive things. His theory, criticised by Aristotle and Theophrastus, is that all things give off effluences and that these enter pores in the sense organs. The pores and the effluences will be of varying shapes and sizes and so only certain effluences enter certain sense-organs if they meet pores of the correct size and shape to admit them. Further, perception is achieved by the attraction of similars. We perceive light colours with fire in the eye, dark colours with water, smell is achieved by the presence of breath in the nostrils etc.

As Theophrastus complains, perception is closely linked to thought by Empedocles

"With earth, we perceive earth, with water, we perceive water, with air divine fire, with destructive fire, with love, we perceive love, and strife with baneful strife. All things are fitted together and constructed out of these, and by means of them they think and feel pleasure and pain."

Empedocles moves from perception of physical elements to ethical perceptions using the same theory of perception by similar, we can see the theory used to account more directly for thought itself. Hence for Empedocles there is a close link between what we perceive and what we think. Further our thoughts will also be affected by our own physical constitutions. This process of the attraction of like to like is operative from the most fundamental level with the parts of the roots of matter being attracted to their like, right up to the highest level of the purest mixture which is the highest form of thought. Hence it seems that everything in nature has a share in perception and intelligence, "know that all things have intelligence and a share of thought."

Conclusion

Empedocles seems to have strongly suggested that people suffer because they have a wrong belief about the nature of existence, thinking that they are born, live, and then cease to exist at death or wander as ghosts in another realm. He maintains that, instead, one returns to essential essence after leaving the body and then returns in another form. In this, his teachings are similar to those of the Buddha who also recognized that suffering is caused by one's ignorance of the nature of existence. Once one grasped the true nature of reality, Buddha claimed, the truth would release one from the cycle of rebirth, death, and suffering.

As noted, more of Empedocles' fragments are extant than those of any other Pre-Socratic philosopher and he is referenced more often by Plato than most others. Plato's famous passage in Symposium, in which the playwright Aristophanes discusses the whole beings which were split apart and ever after search for their other half, is a direct reference to Empedocles' concept of Love and Strife.

His concept of the unified essence of reality inspired the concept of the atomic universe advocated by Leucippus and Democritus, claiming all matter is of a single substance, but also encouraged Gorgias' claim that there was no such thing as "knowledge", only "opinion" and the truth of existence was ultimately unknowable. Empedocles would have disagreed with his student on this in that one only had to accept his vision to understand the universe and one's intimate connection to its eternal essence.

Anaxagoras conceived the origin of the cosmos as the pre-existing, undifferentiated continuum of all material elements of the cosmos. Those elements initially existed in potentiality and were gradually differentiated in the process of development. He explained the process of development as a natural and mechanical one, which is common to the natural philosophy of pre-Socratics. However, unlike other pre-Socratic philosophers, Anaxagoras introduced the idea of Nous, a mind or reason, as the giver of order, purpose, and teleological relationships among things in the cosmos. The Nous, however, remained only as the giver of the initial architecture of the world and did not play any other role. In his dialogue, Plato described Socrates' excitement toward this innovative insight and disappointment at its limited role. Both Plato and Aristotle criticised the lack of ethical elements in his concept of Nous. Anaxagoras brought Ionian philosophy to Athens and gave scientific explanations of natural phenomena. His account of the sun not as a god but as a blazing stone evoked a controversy. He was brought to trial on the charge of impiety. Anaxagoras fled to Lampsacus, a Milesian colony, before being sentenced and died there respected and honoured.

Nous (mind or spirit) as the giver of the order of cosmos

The totality of "seeds" was the material origin of the cosmos. Anaxagoras introduced Nous, mind or reason, which was self-subsisting permanent existence, independent from the material origin of the cosmos; a being that gave order, purpose, and teleological relationships to all beings in the cosmos.

"And whatever they were going to be, and whatever things were then in existence that are not now, and all things that now exist and whatever shall exist—all were arranged by Mind, as also the revolution now followed by the stars, the sun and moon, and the Air and Aether which were separated off." (Fragment 12)

Nous was an architect of the cosmos and the first mover of the cosmic motions that caused diversification of the pre-existing homogeneous material origin. The role of Nous, however, was limited to the cosmogonic starting point, and Anaxagoras explained the development of the cosmos by natural principles.

Anaxagoras's creation of the cosmos

Anaxagoras held that these seeds were eternal and have always been in existence. For Anaxagoras, there was no such thing as a void or empty space. At the beginning of the cosmos, such seeds were initially in one huge mass without shape or form. Through nous, or organising principle, this mass was set in rotary motion. This motion caused the mass to separate out into smaller elements.

Anaxagoras believed the creation of the world was due to this separating of the seeds and by the effect of the spinning motion on these seeds. The formation of the universe or cosmos took place in two stages. First was the revolving process, which separated and then remixed the particles. In this stage, all the dark particles came together to form night, and the fluid seeds joined to make the oceans. The friction in this rotary motion in turn caused heat, which set the stars and sun on fire.

The development of all living things came in the second stage, when the same types of seeds or particles attracted others like them. The separation of the seeds by the rotary motion was imperfect, as Anaxagoras noted, and therefore, according to his theory, there are a few seeds of everything in everything else. What makes something what we believe it to be is that it has a majority of seeds of one type. For example, white is white because it has a majority of white seeds, but it also contains black seeds. Hair is hair, because most of its seeds are of the hair type, but it also has parts of everything else in creation in it.

Ordering the universe and studying it

An important factor of Anaxagoras's theory is the action he claimed nous had upon the organisation of the universe. This approach was popular with later philosophers such as Socrates, Plato, and Aristotle, all of whom were highly concerned with ethical problems and how to live a good life. For them, the concept of an ordering principle to the universe, such as nous, was appealing. They criticised Anaxagoras, however, for not taking his theory further and explaining the purpose of such an ordering principle. Anaxagoras simply explained his theory of matter and motion but did not ask why it happened as it did.

Anaxagoras was also known for his work in astronomy which may have been inspired by the fall of a large meteorite, or mass of matter that falls to Earth from space, near Aegypotomi in 467 BCE. He believed that the sun was a blazing ball of metal about the size of the Peloponessus, the major island of southern Greece. Anaxagoras went further, however, and said that the moon was made of similar matter as Earth and shone because it reflected light from the sun. From this, he went on to describe how Earth moves between the sun and moon, blocking the light and causing lunar eclipses. He also explained how the moon sometimes moves between Earth and sun, causing a solar eclipse.

Effects On Thought

Anaxagoras's work had a significant effect on philosophy and thought. His theory of nous proved an inspiration for Socrates, though the latter was sorry Anaxagoras had not taken his argument further. For Socrates, nous seemed to be simply a mechanical means of organising the universe, a force without morality or goal. Socrates believed there was more than this to the universe. Nevertheless, Anaxagoras's theory of creation is historically important because some of its aspects were adopted by later scientists. These include his theory of the rotating cosmic mass at the beginning of time and his idea that the basic building blocks of life could be divided. More importantly, by attempting to explain the process of creation without relying on gods as the driving factor, Anaxagoras helped to pave the way for criticism of religious ideas about the origin of the universe. His explanation of the formation of heavenly bodies such as the sun, stars, and the moon ultimately led to doubts in God's existence (agnosticism) or possibly even a complete lack of belief in God or gods. Some historians, however, call Anaxagoras the father of theism, the belief in a personal god that created the universe, or even of monotheism, the belief in one supreme being. Although it was never referred to as a god, the nous Anaxagoras believed in was the thing that set the early cosmos in motion and organised life. This was taken by some to mean that Anaxagoras's theory focused on one power or force in the universe, rather than a pantheon, or group, of gods as the Greeks had believed. Therefore, the father of agnosticism or atheism is sometimes also called the father of monotheism.

Conclusion

Anaxagoras, however, seems to believe his Mind concept needs no further development because its role is self-evident: it set perceivable reality in motion from a state of unity and therefore answers Parmenides and Zeno. The universe is of a single substance but change and motion are possible through the "mingling" of substances which, when their present form breaks apart, separate to take another form. Mind was the architect of this design and, once completed, did not need to participate further. In answer to Zeno's Racecourse, then, one would be able to move from Point A to Point Z in a Monist universe through the mingling and separation of essential essence which allows for what people define as "motion" and "change".

Anaxagoras continued to teach at Athens until he was charged with impiety in c. 450 BCE for denying the sun and moon were deities, claiming instead they were rocks. The charges may have stemmed from his close association with Pericles whose political enemies decided to attack the teacher to harm his student. Pericles spoke in Anaxagoras' defense, and he was allowed to pay a fine, rather than face a trial and possible execution, and he retired to Lampasacus in Troad (modern-day Turkey) where he lived out the rest of his life as a highly respected philosopher and teacher.

Atomism

Atomism is a natural philosophy rooted in ancient Greece that states the universe is made up of indestructible particles known as atoms. The earliest known Atomists are the ancient Greek philosophers Leucippus and Democritus. The words 'atomism' and 'atoms' derive from the Greek word 'atomos', meaning uncuttable.

Leucippus and Democritus

Leucippus was a pre-Socratic natural philosopher who lived in ancient Greece during the fifth century BCE. Little is known about the man himself, but he is credited as the philosopher to first develop the theory of atomism. Diogenes Laertius, a biographer of Greek philosophers who lived during the third century CE, recorded that Leucippus was a student of Zeno. Zeno was a philosopher who came from the Eleatic school of thought; his teachings focus on the paradox that motion does not exist but is merely an illusion. His argument is that because size and distance can be divided an infinite number of times, it is impossible to traverse any distance because it would, in turn, take an infinite amount of time.

Leucippus' atomism is thought to be a response to Zeno's theory because atoms are the last level by which matter can be divided; therefore, distance cannot be divided an infinite number of times. This explains how motion can exist and refutes the thought that motion would take an infinite amount of time. Only fragments of Leucippus' writings have survived; it is solely through the writings of Leucippus' student Democritus that his theory is fully explained.

Leucippus' and Democritus' Atomic Model

According to Leucippus and Democritus, the basis for the atomic model is that the universe is made up of two fundamental elements: atoms and the void. Atoms are the smallest division of matter, making them indestructible and composing all physical objects. The void is the absence of matter; it is the space that exists between atoms.

In this system of two elements, change only occurs at the level of appearances. Atoms themselves do not change. Only the form they take changes. The different combinations and shapes of atoms form to create the differences in physical objects and beings. They did not believe that atoms themselves could be different.

Democritus and Leucippus also use this model to explain the creation of the universe or the cosmos. According to their theories, when atoms group into a cosmic whirlpool, they create a force that starts a fire that settles into the form of a star. The outer membrane of the whirl continues to collect atoms, which in turn construct planets.

Atoms and the Void

Like Anaxagoras and Empedocles, the Atomists claimed that there was a level of reality that satisfied the Eleatic demands. This level of reality was populated by atoms and the void. Atoms are, literally, indivisible particles, which are so small that they can be split no further. The atoms qualify as Parmenidean Reals in two ways. First, like the four elements and the homeomeric substances, atoms cannot be generated, destroyed, or qualitatively changed. In addition, they have an added level of compliance with the Parmenidean demands: the atoms themselves are one in kind. All atoms are made out of the same material. Reality, then, really is one and continuous in at least a qualitative sense.

Though the atoms are materially homogenous, they do have some variable properties. They differ from one another in shape, arrangement, position, size, and motion. It is by the arrangement and rearrangement of atoms of different shapes, sizes, and motions that the observable world comes into being.

The boldest aspect of the atomist theory is that, in addition to positing the atoms as Parmenidean Reals, it also posits a void, which is identified explicitly with non-being. There is an extremely good reason for this move: the Eleatics argued that (1) being cannot admit of a vacuum and (2) without a vacuum there can be no movement. Leucippus was impressed by both of these arguments and was persuaded of their truth. However, he was equally certain of the truth of the claim that movement does in fact exist, since he saw movement all around him. Reasoning with these three premises he concluded that there must actually be a vacuum and that this vacuum must be identified with not-being. Though the vacuum is non-being, it is nonetheless real. The atoms exist in this vacuum or void and move about in it, giving rise to the observable world.

Unlike his Eleatic teachers, Leucippus was apparently not overly concerned about mixing the ideas of being and not-being, nor about talking about not-being. As far as we know, he did not take the further step, which would soon be taken by Plato, and make gestures at diffusing this worry, by distinguishing between grades of being and types of negation.

The Visible World

In order to account for the phenomena of the observable world, the atomists tell a detailed story about the coming together and separation of atoms in the void. Through their motion, the atoms collide, and though they never really touch, they form objects through their close association. The nature of these objects depends on the variable properties of the atoms thus joined, their arrangement, size, shape, and motion. Once again, then, what looks like generation, destruction, and change in the observable world, is really not a violation of the Eleatic demands; all that really exists in the most fundamental sense are arrangements of atoms in the void.

Using this theory of atoms in the void, the atomists are the first philosophers to venture a full-fledged theory of sensation. They attempt to explain all of the macroscopic qualities of the world by appealing only to the size, shape, order, and position of atoms.

An excellent example of this attempt is Democritus's account of taste. The sensations of taste, he explains, are entirely a function of the size and shape of atoms in food and their interaction with the atoms of our mouths. Sour taste, he tells us, is the result of angular atoms in twisted configurations. Sweet taste, on the other hand, is caused by rounded atoms of a moderate size. Astringent tastes come from large, barely circular atoms with many angles. Finally, bitter tastes are caused by small, smooth, round atoms, with no hooks on their surfaces. All foods, in fact, have a mixture of all of these sorts of atoms, but it is the predominant sort in the mixture that we perceive most clearly. In effect, what Democritus has done with this account, is to reduce taste to visual and tactile terms. He gives a similarly detailed account of our sensation of colour, explaining this phenomenon on the basis of the size and shape of atoms, as well as the nature of the void between them.

Atomism in the Enlightenment and Beyond

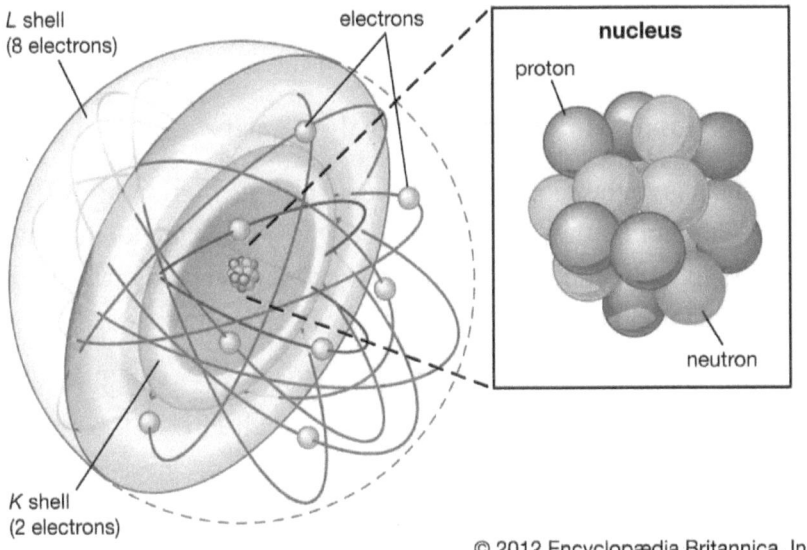

© 2012 Encyclopædia Britannica, Inc.

Despite the fate of the likes of Bruno, interest in atomism survived well into the 17th century and beyond. Unlike ancient atomism, the growing scientific movement of the Enlightenment was generally more interested in 'mechanical atomism'. Rather than using atomism to explore the nature of the soul, celestial beings and so on, mechanical atomists preferred to apply their theories to the material world around them.

Like so many theories before them, mechanical atomism also believed that the world was composed entirely of atoms moving through the void. Atoms were still changeless and mechanical atomists still viewed them as the smallest element of matter. Isaac Newton's work on forces were incorporated into explanations of the properties of these atoms, but philosophers and scientists struggled to prove their theories via empirical experiments.

Since then, atomism has continued to inspire various thinkers and scientists. It has appeared in research on thermodynamics and kinetic theory in the 19th century, as well as early 20th century theories on particle motion. Although there are obviously vast differences in context and theory between ancient philosophical atomism and modern-day atomic theory, it's still amazing to think that people like Democritus were 'proved right' about their ideas to a certain degree!

Nature of Atomic Motion and Physical Necessity

The atomists give the most detailed account of the motion of their real entities. The atoms, they tell us, move by a jostling, random motion that occurs by collision. Motion, on this view, as on many later views, is transmitted upon collision.

The motion of the atoms is eternal and involves no external forces like love, strife, or mind. Instead, the motion, and all else in the physical world, is supposed to be explained by the notion of "necessity." The claim that everything happens by necessity can be seen as a very primitive (and not very well thought out, it seems) form of modern determinism—the view that every event is an effect of some prior series of effects. The order of the cosmos, then, is not imposed by some outside force on the atomist view. In modern terms we would say that order prevails in the atomist view because it falls out of the laws of nature, which govern the atoms. Another way to put this is to say that the ultimate controlling principle in nature is that everything follows the laws of its own being. But the atomist notion of necessity probably did not take this sophisticated form, drawing on the concept of natural law. A more accurate description of their notion of necessity would only assert that X determines some future Y because X has the proper atoms, plus the suitable motion, to yield Y and only Y. This form of determinism is very weak, so weak that it cannot really be made to work; there is nothing else in the system to explain why X would determine Y and only Y, since there is no idea of natural law.

The Sophists were orators, public speakers, mouths for hire in an oral culture. They were gifted with speech. They were skilled in what becomes known as Rhetoric. They were respected, feared and hated. They had a gift and used it in a manner that aroused the ire of many. They challenged, questioned, and did not care to arrive at the very best answers. They cared about winning public speaking contests, debates, and lawsuits, and in charging fees to teach others how to do as they did. To be able to speak well meant a great deal at that time. As there was no real paper available, there were no written contracts or deeds and disputes that would be settled today with a set of documents as evidence back then they would need to be settled through a contest of words: one person's words against another's. Whoever presented the best oral case would often prevail. To speak well was very important. The Sophists were very good speakers. Indeed, they had reputations for being able to convince a crowd that up was down, that day was night, that the wrong answer could be the right answer, that good was bad and bad is good, even that injustice is justice and justice would be made to appear as injustice!

To support one's position in any matter, nothing better could be offered than a quotation from one of the works, which told of the gods and their actions. If an action of the gods could be found that was similar to that being taken by a party to a debate, then that was evidence of the correctness of that action. Therefore, those who were the fastest and most accurate at being able to locate quotations and take them and apply them to a given situation would often win the debate, the contest, the lawsuit or discussion. The Sophists were very well versed in the epic tales and poems. They were able to find the most appropriate quotation to support any position. They regularly entered contests and those who won were given prizes, but no prize was greater than being the victor and able to charge the highest rates of tuition to instruct the sons of the wealthy in how to speak in public. This skill was needed to defend oneself against lawsuits even against the most frivolous of lawsuits brought by one who thought himself to be the better speaker.

The Sophists taught courses that might have been labelled with such current phrasings as:

- How to win no matter how bad your case is.
- How to win friends and influence people
- How to succeed in business without really trying
- How to fall into a pigsty and come out smelling like a rose.
- How to succeed in life.
- How to play to win

The Sophists held no values other than winning and succeeding. They were not true believers in the myths of the Greeks but would use references and quotations from the tales for their own purposes. They were secular atheists, relativists and cynical about religious beliefs and all traditions. They believed and taught that "might makes right". They were pragmatists trusting in whatever works to bring about the desired end at whatever the cost. They made a business of their own form of education as developing skills in rhetoric and profited from it.

Their concerns were not with truth but with practical knowledge. They practised rhetoric in order to persuade and not to discover the truth. Their art was to persuade the crowd and not to convince people of the truth. They moved thought from cosmology and cosmogony and theogony, stories of the gods and the universe, to a concern for humanity. Their focus was human civilization and human customs. Their theatre was the ethical and political problems of immediate concern for humans. They put the individual human being at the centre of all thought and value. They did not hold for any universals, not universal truths nor universal values. They sought and took payment for their lessons at speaking and writing

PROTOGORAS

Protagoras was born about 481 BCE at Abdera in Thrace. He is believed to have come to Athens sometime by the middle of the century. Pericles entrusted him with the task of drawing up a constitution for the colony of Thurio, founded in 444 BCE. He was back at Athens in 431 and during the plague in 430 which killed two of Pericles' sons. The story goes that Protagoras was charged with blasphemy because of his book on the gods, fled the country before trial, and was drowned on the crossing to Sicily.

PRODICUS

Prodicus was a native of the island of Ceos in the Aegean. Like most of his compatriots, he is said to have possessed a pessimistic disposition. In the pseudo-Platonic dialogue Axiochus it is said that he considered death desirable as it afforded an escape from the evils of life. Fear of death, he argued, is irrational because death concerns neither the living nor the dead. The basis of this argument is the notion that life and death are mutually exclusive. Prodicus' chief contribution was in the area of theogony. In the beginning men worshipped natural objects – sun, moon, rivers, lakes, fruits etc. - as gods because these were useful to them. The cult of the Nile in Egypt was an example of this practice. The next stage was worship of inventors of various arts and crafts – agriculture, viniculture, metal work etc. So, they had such deities like Demeter, Dionysus, Hephaestus. This view rendered prayer superfluous and for this reason, Prodicus got into trouble with authorities at Athens. Like Protagoras, Prodicus too was interested in the study of language. He wrote a treatise on synonyms. His style was markedly pedantic.

HIPPIAS

A younger contemporary of Protagoras, Hippias of Elis was a polymath, being well versed in mathematics, astronomy, grammar and rhetoric, music, literature, history and mythology. He prided himself on his sartorial skills. His list of the Olympic victors paved the way for the later Greek system of dating by means of the Olympiads. In the Protagoras, Plato attributes to him the view that law is the tyrant of men, which forces them to do many things contrary to nature. It appears that Hippias wanted to draw attention to laws of the city state that were at variance with natural laws.

GORGIAS

Gorgias visited Athens in 427 BCE as the leader of an embassy from Leontini, with the successful intention of persuading the Athenians to make an alliance against Syracuse. He travelled extensively around Greece, earning large sums of money by giving lessons in rhetoric and epideictic speeches.

Plato's gorgias depicts the rhetorician as something of a celebrity, who either does not have well thought out views on the implications of his expertise, or is reluctant to share them, and who denies his responsibility for the unjust use of rhetorical skill by errant students. Although Gorgias presents himself as moderately upstanding, the dramatic structure of Plato's dialogue suggests that the defense of injustice by Polus and the appeal to the natural right of the stronger by Callicles are partly grounded in the conceptual presuppositions of Gorgianic rhetoric.

THE LESSER SOPHISTS

Amongst the lesser figures of the Sophist movement one might mention Callimachus who put forward the 'might is right' doctrine; Lycophron who asserted that nobility is a sham, that all men are equal; Thrasymachus of Chalcedon who figures in the Republic as the brutal champion of the rights of the stronger; and Antiphon of Athens who denounced the distinction between nobles and commons, Greeks and barbarians as itself a barbarism.

Modern Usage

While a particular bad and insincere argument is likely to be labelled a sophism the practice of using such arguments is known as sophistry. In its modern meaning, "sophistry" is a derogatory term for rhetoric that is designed to appeal to the listener on grounds other than the strict logical cogency of the statements being made.

In traditional logical argument, a set of premises are connected together according to the rules of logic and lead therefore to some conclusion.

When someone criticises the argument, they do so by pointing out either falsehoods among the premises or logical fallacies, flaws in the logical scaffolding. These criticisms may be subject to countercriticisms, which in turn may be subject to counter-countercriticisms, etc. Generally, some judge or audience eventually either concurs with or rejects the position of one side and thus a consensus opinion of the truth arrived upon.

The essential claim of sophistry is that the actual logical validity of an argument is irrelevant; it is only the ruling of the audience that ultimately determines whether a conclusion is considered "true" or not. By appealing to the prejudices and emotions of the judges, one can garner favourable treatment for one's side of the argument and cause a factually false position to be ruled true.

The philosophical Sophist goes one step beyond that and claims that since it was traditionally accepted that the position ruled valid by the judges was literally true, any position ruled true by the judges must be considered literally true, even if it was arrived at by naked pandering to the judges' prejudices — or even by bribery.

Critics would argue that this claim relies on a straw man caricature of logical discourse and is, in fact, a self-justifying act of sophistry.

Philosophy

Philosophical perspectives of sophists were critically exposed and analysed by Plato. Although all sophists may not have shared the same view, Plato depicted their general perspective.

Scepticism and relativism

Sophists travelled and witnessed diverse views of God and customs, and developed relativistic or antagonistic views for religious faith, morality, and values. They presented a skeptical or critical or antagonistic view to the existence of an absolute, permanent, and objective standard of truth. They viewed truth or a standard of good and evil as a matter of interpretation. A major sophist, Protagoras' phrase, "man is the measure of all things" indicates this relativistic view of truth.

If there is no objective standard of truth we can appeal to or can determine the validity of claims, arguments become like a game or a battle where winning or losing is at stake and rhetorical skills become a definitive universal tool.

Might is right

In the absence of the objective standard of truth or right and wrong, the perspective of "might is right" emerged. Thrasymachus, another prominent sophist, developed this view. Citing historical cases, he challenged Socrates and explained how winners in fact defined and determined justice and judged losers according to the standard they set. Thrasymachus held a view that power determines and defines good and evil. Even deceptive measures were justified as far as they serve for winning over opponents. This power-based value perspective entails a nihilistic view of life. One may also find an incipient idea of Machiavellianism.

The ancient notion of nomos as divine laws that dominated both gods and humans were no longer present in Callicles' thought. There was no permanent or absolute principle such as divine justice that abided human society.

Reality and Appearance

If winning or losing is the essential matter, how one appears or looks to others becomes far more important than how one in fact is. Due to the denial of the existence of unchanging, permanent truth or reality, the world is dissolved and reduced to only appearance or phenomena. In Plato's terms, Sophists stressed the importance of "appearance" over "reality," "opinion" over "knowledge," or eradicated their distinction since the world is theoretically limited to appearance in a sophist worldview.

Secular conception of happiness

Sophists often identified happiness with pleasure and promoted secular materialistic social success. In their view, happiness can be achieved and joy can be experienced without moral goodness. Plato challenged and argued that human beings cannot experience genuine joy and happiness without being morally good. Kant also argued that moral goodness was the condition for happiness.

While sophists defined joy as all forms of pleasure in general, Plato distinguished joy, pleasure, and happiness in two modes: authentic and inauthentic, or genuine and false. Sophists missed this distinction in their analyses of human nature and life.

The Sophists carried on their work of instruction by the education of the young and by giving popular lectures in the cities; but as they were itinerant professors, men of wide experience, and representative of a, as yet, somewhat sceptical and superficial reaction, the idea became current that they gathered together the young men from their homes and then pulled to pieces before them the traditional ethical code and religious beliefs. Accordingly, the strict adherents of tradition regarded the Sophists with some suspicion, though the young were their enthusiastic supporters. Not that the levelling-out tendencies of the Sophists were all weakening to Greek life: their breadth of view generally made them advocates of Panhellenism, a doctrine sorely needed in the Greece of the city-state. But it was their sceptical tendencies that attracted most attention, especially as they did not put anything really new and stable in place of the old convictions which they tended to unsettle. To this should be added the fact that they took payment for the instruction which they imparted. This practice, however legitimate in itself, was at variance with the practice of the older Greek philosophers, and did not agree with the Greek opinion of what was fitting. It was abhorrent to Plato, while Xenophon says that the Sophists speak and write to deceive for their gain, and they give no help to anyone.

From what has been said, it is clear that Sophism does not deserve any sweeping condemnation. By turning the attention of thinkers to man himself, the thinking and willing subject, it served as a transition stage to the great Platonic-Aristotelian achievement. In affording a means of training and instruction, it fulfilled a necessary task in the political life of Greece, while its Panhellenistic tendencies certainly stand to its credit. And even its skeptical and relativist tendencies, which were, after all, largely the result of the breakdown of the older philosophy on the one hand, and of a wider experience of human life on the other, at least contributed to the raising of problems, even if Sophism itself was unable to solve these problems. It is not fanciful to discern the influence of Sophism in the Greek drama, in Sophocles' hymn to human achievement in the Antigone and in the theoretical discussions contained in the plays of Euripides, and in the works of the Greek historians, in the celebrated Melian dialogue in the pages of Thucydides. The term Σοφιστής took some time to acquire its disparaging connotation. The name is applied by Herodotus to Solon and Pythagoras, by Androtion to the Seven Wise Men and to Socrates, by Lysias to Plato. Moreover, the older Sophists won for themselves general respect and esteem, and, as historians have pointed out, were not infrequently selected as "ambassadors" of their respective cities, a fact which hardly points to their being or being regarded as charlatans. It was only secondarily that the term "Sophist" acquired an unsavoury flavour — as in Plato; and in later times the term seems to have reacquired a good sense, being applied to the professors of rhetoric and prose writers of the Empire, without the significance of quibbler or cheat. "It is particularly through the opposition to Socrates and Plato that the Sophists have come into such disrepute that the word now usually signifies that, by false reasoning, some truth is either refuted and made dubious, or something false is proved and made plausible."

On the other hand, the relativism of the Sophists, their encouragement of Eristic, their lack of stable norms, their acceptance of pay, and the hair-splitting tendencies of certain later Sophists, justify to a great extent the disparaging signification of the term. For Plato, they are "shopkeepers with spiritual wares"; and when Socrates is represented in the Protagoras as asking Hippocrates, who wanted to receive instruction from Protagoras, "Wouldn't you be ashamed to show yourself to the Greeks as a Sophist?"

Hippocrates answers: "Yes, truly, Socrates, if I am to say what I think." We must, however, remember that Plato tends to bring out the bad side of the Sophists, largely because he had Socrates before his eyes, who had developed what was good in Sophism beyond all comparison with the achievements of the Sophists themselves.

The philosopher Socrates an enigma, an inscrutable individual who, despite having written nothing, is considered one of the handful of philosophers who forever changed how philosophy itself was to be conceived. All our information about him is second-hand and most of it vigorously disputed, but his trial and death at the hands of the Athenian democracy is nevertheless the founding myth of the academic discipline of philosophy. His influence has been felt far beyond philosophy itself, and in every age. Because his life is widely considered paradigmatic not only for the philosophic life but, more generally, for how anyone ought to live, Socrates has been encumbered with the adulation and emulation ordinarily reserved for religious figures – strange for someone who tried so hard to make others do their own thinking and for someone convicted and executed on the charge of irreverence toward the gods. Certainly, he was impressive — so impressive that many others were moved to write about him, all of whom found him strange by the conventions of fifth-century Athens: in his appearance, personality, and behaviour, as well as in his views and methods.

Socrates's strangeness

Standards of beauty are different in different eras, and in Socrates's time, beauty could easily be measured by the standard of the gods. Stately, proportionate sculptures of gods had been adorning the Athenian acropolis since about the time Socrates reached the age of thirty. Good looks and proper bearing were important to a man's political prospects, for beauty and goodness were linked in the popular imagination. The extant sources agree that Socrates was profoundly ugly, resembling a satyr more than a man—and resembling not at all the statues that turned up later in ancient times and now grace Internet sites and the covers of books. He had wide-set, bulging eyes that darted sideways and enabled him, like a crab, to see not only what was straight ahead, but what was beside him as well; a flat, upturned nose with flaring nostrils; and large fleshy lips. Socrates let his hair grow long, Spartan-style, and went about barefoot and unwashed, carrying a stick and looking arrogant. He didn't change his clothes but efficiently wore in the daytime what he covered himself with at night. Something was peculiar about his gait as well, sometimes described as a swagger so intimidating that enemy soldiers kept their distance. He was impervious to the effects of alcohol and cold weather, but this made him an object of suspicion to his fellow soldiers on campaign. We can safely assume an average height, and a strong build, given the active life he appears to have led. Against the iconic tradition of a potbelly, Socrates and his companions are described as going hungry.

In the late fifth century BCE, it was more or less taken for granted that any self-respecting Athenian male would prefer fame, wealth, honours, and political power to a life of labour. Although many citizens lived by their labour in a wide variety of occupations, they were expected to spend much of their leisure time, if they had any, busying themselves with the affairs of the city. Men regularly participated in the governing Assembly and in the city's many courts; and those who could afford it prepared themselves for success at public life by studying with rhetoricians and sophists from abroad who could themselves become wealthy and famous by teaching the young men of Athens to use words to their advantage. Other forms of higher education were also known in Athens: mathematics, astronomy, geometry, music, ancient history, and linguistics. One of the things that seemed strange about Socrates is that he neither laboured to earn a living, nor participated voluntarily in affairs of state. Rather, he embraced poverty and, although youths of the city kept company with him and imitated him, Socrates adamantly insisted he was not a teacher and refused all his life to take money for what he did. The strangeness of this behaviour is mitigated by the image then current of teachers and students: teachers were viewed as pitchers pouring their contents into the empty cups that were the students. Because Socrates was no transmitter of information that others were passively to receive, he resists the comparison to teachers. Rather, he helped others recognize on their own what is real, true, and good— a new, and thus suspect, approach to education. He was known for confusing, stinging, and stunning his conversation partners into the unpleasant experience of realising their own ignorance, a state sometimes superseded by genuine intellectual curiosity.

It did not help matters that Socrates seemed to have a higher opinion of women than most of his companions had, speaking of "men and women," "priests and priestesses," likening his work to midwifery, and naming foreign women as his teachers: Socrates claimed to have learned rhetoric from Aspasia of Miletus, the de facto spouse of Peric and to have learned erotics from the priestess Diotima of Mantinea. Socrates was unconventional in a related respect. Athenian citizen males of the upper social classes did not marry until they were at least thirty, and Athenian females were poorly educated and kept sequestered until puberty, when they were given in marriage by their fathers. Thus, the socialisation and education of males often involved a relationship for which the English word 'pederasty' is misleading, in which a youth approaching manhood, fifteen to seventeen, became the beloved of a male lover a few years older, under whose tutelage and through whose influence and gifts, the younger man would be guided and improved. It was assumed among Athenians that mature men would find youths sexually attractive, and such relationships were conventionally viewed as beneficial to both parties by family and friends alike. A degree of hypocrisy, however, was implied by the arrangement: "officially" it did not involve sexual relations between the lovers and, if it did, then the beloved was not supposed to derive pleasure from the act—but ancient evidence shows that both restrictions were often violated. What was odd about Socrates is that, although he was no exception to the rule of finding youths attractive, he refused the physical advances of even his favourite, Alcibiades, and kept his eye on the improvement of their, and all the Athenians', a mission he said he had been assigned by the oracle of Apollo at Delphi, if he was interpreting his friend Chaerephon's report correctly , a preposterous claim in the eyes of his fellow citizens. Socrates also acknowledged a rather strange personal phenomenon, a daimonion or internal voice that prohibited his doing certain things, some trivial and some important, often unrelated to matters of right and wrong (thus not to be confused with the popular notions of a superego or a conscience). The implication that he was guided by something he regarded as divine or semi-divine was all the more reason for other Athenians to be suspicious of Socrates.

Socrates was usually to be found in the marketplace and other public areas, conversing with a variety of different people—young and old, male and female, slave and free, rich and poor, citizen and visitor—that is, with virtually anyone he could persuade to join with him in his question-and-answer mode of probing serious matters. Socrates's lifework consisted in the examination of people's lives, his own and others', because "the unexamined life is not worth living for a human being," as he says at his trial. Socrates pursued this task single-mindedly, questioning people about what matters most, e.g., courage, love, reverence, moderation, and the state of their souls generally. He did this regardless of whether his respondents wanted to be questioned or resisted him. Athenian youths imitate Socrates's questioning style, much to the annoyance of some of their elders. He had a reputation for irony, though what that means exactly is controversial; at a minimum, Socrates's irony consisted in his saying that he knew nothing of importance and wanted to listen to others, yet keeping the upper hand in every discussion. One further aspect of Socrates's much-touted strangeness should be mentioned: his dogged failure to align himself politically with oligarchs or democrats; rather, he had friends and enemies among both, and he supported and opposed actions of both.

Who was Socrates?

Socrates was born in Athens in the year 469 BCE to Sophroniscus, a stonemason, and Phaenarete, a midwife. His family was not extremely poor, but they were by no means wealthy, and Socrates could not claim that he was of noble birth like Plato. He grew up in the political deme or district of Alopece, and when he turned 18, began to perform the typical political duties required of Athenian males. These included compulsory military service and membership in the Assembly, the governing body responsible for determining military strategy and legislation.

In a culture that worshipped male beauty, Socrates had the misfortune of being born incredibly ugly. Socrates was exophthalmic, meaning that his eyes bulged out of his head and were not straight but focused sideways. He had a snub nose, which made him resemble a pig, and many sources depict him with a potbelly. Socrates did little to help his odd appearance, frequently wearing the same cloak and sandals throughout both the day and the evening. Plato's *Symposium* offers us one of the few accounts of his caring for his appearance.

As a young man, Socrates was given an education appropriate for a person of his station. By the middle of the 5th century BCE, all Athenian males were taught to read and write. Sophroniscus, however, also took pains to give his son an advanced cultural education in poetry, music, and athletics. In both Plato and Xenophon, we find a Socrates that is well versed in poetry, talented at music, and quite at-home in the gymnasium. In accordance with Athenian custom, his father also taught him a trade, though Socrates did not labour at it on a daily basis. Rather, he spent his days in the agora, asking questions of those who would speak with him. While he was poor, he quickly acquired a following of rich young aristocrats one of whom Plato was, who particularly enjoyed hearing him interrogate those that were purported to be the wisest and most influential men in the city.

Socrates was married to Xanthippe, and according to some sources, had a second wife. Most suggest that he first married Xanthippe, and that she gave birth to his first son, Lamprocles. He is alleged to have married his second wife, Myrto, without dowry, and she gave birth to his other two sons, Sophroniscus and Menexenus. Various accounts attribute Sophroniscus to Xanthippe, while others even suggest that Socrates was married to both women simultaneously because of a shortage of males in Athens at the time. In accordance with Athenian custom, Socrates was open about his physical attraction to young men, though he always subordinated his physical desire for them to his desire that they improve the condition of their souls.

Socrates fought valiantly during his time in the Athenian military. Just before the Peloponnesian War with Sparta began in 431 BCE, he helped the Athenians win the battle of Potidaea (432 BCE), after which he saved the life of Alcibiades, the famous Athenian general. He also fought as one of 7,000 hoplites aside 20,000 troops at the battle of Delium (424 BCE) and once more at the battle of Amphipolis (422 BCE). Both battles were defeats for Athens.

Despite his continued service to his city, many members of Athenian society perceived Socrates to be a threat to their democracy, and it is this suspicion that largely contributed to his conviction in court. It is therefore imperative to understand the historical context in which his trial was set.

The Threat to Democracy

While many of his fellow citizens found considerable evidence against Socrates, there was also historical evidence in addition to his military service for the case that he was not just a passive but an active supporter of democracy. For one thing, just as he had associates that were known oligarchs, he also had associates that were supporters of the democracy, including the metic family of Cephalus and Socrates' friend Chaerephon, the man who reported that the oracle at Delphi had proclaimed that no man was wiser than Socrates. Additionally, when he was ordered by the Thirty to help retrieve the democratic general Leon from the island of Salamis for execution, he refused to do so. His refusal could be understood not as the defiance of a legitimately established government but rather his allegiance to the ideals of due process that were in effect under the previously instituted democracy. Indeed, in Plato's Crito, Socrates refuses to escape from prison on the grounds that he lived his whole life with an implied agreement with the laws of the democracy.

Greek Religion and Socrates' Impiety

Because of the amnesty the charges made against Socrates were framed in religious terms. "Socrates does criminal wrong by not recognizing the gods that the city recognizes, and furthermore by introducing new divinities; and he also does criminal wrong by corrupting the youth". Many people understood the charge about corrupting the youth to signify that Socrates taught his subversive views to others, a claim that he adamantly denies in his defense speech by claiming that he has no wisdom to teach and that he cannot be held responsible for the actions of those that heard him speak.

It is now customary to refer to the principal written accusation on the deposition submitted to the Athenian court as an accusation of impiety, or unholiness. Rituals, ceremonies, and sacrifices that were officially sanctioned by the city and its officials marked ancient Greek religion. The sacred was woven into the everyday experience of citizens who demonstrated their piety by correctly observing their ancestral traditions. Interpretation of the gods at their temples was the exclusive domain of priests appointed and recognized by the city. The boundary and separation between the religious and the secular that we find in many countries today therefore did not obtain in Athens. A religious crime was consequently an offence not just against the gods, but also against the city itself.

Socrates and his contemporaries lived in a polytheistic society, a society in which the gods did not create the world but were themselves created. Socrates would have been brought up with the stories of the gods recounted in Hesiod and Homer, in which the gods were not omniscient, omnibenevolent, or eternal, but rather power-hungry super-creatures that regularly intervened in the affairs of human beings. Human beings were to fear the gods, sacrifice to them, and honour them with festivals and prayers.

Socrates instead seemed to have a conception of the divine as always benevolent, truthful, authoritative, and wise. For him, divinity always operated in accordance with the standards of rationality. This conception of divinity, however, dispenses with the traditional conception of prayer and sacrifice as motivated by hopes for material payoff. Socrates' theory of the divine seemed to make the most important rituals and sacrifices in the city entirely useless, for if the gods are all good, they will benefit human beings regardless of whether or not human beings make offerings to them. Jurors at his trial might have thought that, without the expectation of material reward or protection from the gods, Socrates was disconnecting religion from its practical roots and its connection with the civic identity of the city.

While Socrates was critical of blind acceptance of the gods and the myths we find in Hesiod and Homer, this in itself was not unheard of in Athens at the time. Solon, Xenophanes, Heraclitus, and Euripides had all spoken against the capriciousness and excesses of the gods without incurring penalty. It is possible to make the case that Socrates' jurors might not have indicted him solely on questioning the gods or even on interrogating the true meaning of piety. Indeed, there was no legal definition of piety in Athens at the time, and jurors were therefore in a similar situation to the one in which we find Socrates in Plato's Euthyphro, that is, in need of an inquiry into what the nature of piety truly is. What seems to have concerned the jurors was not only Socrates' challenge to the traditional interpretation of the gods of the city, but his seeming allegiance to an entirely novel divine being, unfamiliar to anyone in the city.

Whereas in Plato's Apology Socrates makes no attempt to reconcile his divine sign with traditional views of piety, Xenophon's Socrates argues that just as there are those who rely on bird calls and receive guidance from voices, so he too is influenced by his daimon. However, Socrates had no officially sanctioned religious role in the city. As such, his attempt to assimilate himself to a seer or necromancer appointed by the city to interpret divine signs actually may have undermined his innocence, rather than help to establish it. His insistence that he had direct, personal access to the divine made him appear guilty to enough jurors that he was sentenced to death.

How Did Socrates Do Philosophy?

As famous as the Socratic themes are, the Socratic method is equally famous. Socrates conducted his philosophical activity by means of question and answer, and we typically associate with him a method called the elenchus. At the same time, Plato's Socrates calls himself a midwife—who has no ideas of his own but helps give birth to the ideas of others—and proceeds dialectically—defined either as asking questions, embracing the practice of collection and division, or proceeding from hypotheses to first principles.

The Elenchus: Socrates the Refuter

A typical Socratic elenchus is a cross-examination of a particular position, proposition, or definition, in which Socrates tests what his interlocutor says and refutes it. There is, however, great debate amongst scholars regarding not only what is being refuted but also whether the elenchus can prove anything. There are questions, in other words, about the topic of the elenchus and its purpose or goal.

i. Topic

Socrates typically begins his elenchus with the question, "What is it"? What is piety, he asks Euthyphro. Euthyphro appears to give five separate definitions of piety: piety is proceeding against whomever does injustice, piety is what is loved by the gods, piety is what is loved by all the gods, the godly and the pious is the part of the just that is concerned with the care of the gods, and piety is the knowledge of sacrificing and praying. For some commentators, what Socrates is searching for here is a definition. Other commentators argue that Socrates is searching for more than just the definition of piety but seeks a comprehensive account of the nature of piety. Whatever the case, Socrates refutes the answer given to him in response to the 'what is it' question.

Another reading of the Socratic elenchus is that Socrates is not just concerned with the reply of the interlocutor but is concerned with the interlocutor himself. According to this view, Socrates is as much concerned with the truth or falsity of propositions as he is with the refinement of the interlocutor's way of life. Socrates is concerned with both epistemological and moral advances for the interlocutor and himself. It is not propositions or replies alone that are refuted, for Socrates does not conceive of them dwelling in isolation from those that hold them. Thus conceived, the elenchus refutes the person holding a particular view, not just the view. For instance, Socrates shames Thrasymachus when he shows him that he cannot maintain his view that justice is ignorance and injustice is wisdom. The elenchus demonstrates that Thrasymachus cannot consistently maintain all his claims about the nature of justice. This view is consistent with a view we find in Plato's late dialogue called the Sophist, in which the Visitor from Elea, not Socrates, claims that the soul will not get any advantage from learning that it is offered to it until someone shames it by refuting it.

ii. Purpose

In terms of goal, there are two common interpretations of the elenchus. Both have been developed by scholars in response to what Gregory Vlastos called the problem of the Socratic elenchus. The problem is how Socrates can claim that position W is false, when the only thing he has established is its inconsistency with other premises whose truth he has not tried to establish in the elenchus.

The first response is what is called the constructivist position. A constructivist argues that the elenchus establishes the truth or falsity of individual answers. The elenchus on this interpretation can and does have positive results. Vlastos himself argued that Socrates not only established the inconsistency of the interlocutor's beliefs by showing their inconsistency, but that Socrates' own moral beliefs were always consistent, able to withstand the test of the elenchus. Socrates could therefore pick out a faulty premise in his elenctic exchange with an interlocutor and sought to replace the interlocutor's false beliefs with his own.

The second response is called the non-constructivist position. This position claims that Socrates does not think the elenchus can establish the truth or falsity of individual answers. The non-constructivist argues that all the elenchus can show is the inconsistency of W with the premises X, Y, and Z. It cannot establish that ~W is the case, or, for that matter, replace any of the premises with another, for this would require a separate argument. The elenchus establishes the falsity of the conjunction of W, X, Y, and Z, but not the truth or falsity of any of those premises individually. The purpose of the elenchus on this interpretation is to show the interlocutor that he is confused, and, according to some scholars, to use that confusion as a stepping stone on the way to establishing a more consistent, well-formed set of beliefs.

Maieutic: Socrates the Midwife

In Plato's Theaetetus Socrates identifies himself as a midwife. While the dialogue is not generally considered Socratic, it is elenctic insofar as it tests and refutes Theaetetus' definitions of knowledge. It also ends without a conclusive answer to its question, a characteristic it shares with a number of Socratic dialogues.

Socrates tells Theaetetus that his mother Phaenarete was a midwife and that he himself is an intellectual midwife. Whereas the craft of midwifery brings on labour pains or relieves them in order to help a woman deliver a child, Socrates does not watch over the body but over the soul, and helps his interlocutor give birth to an idea. He then applies the elenchus to test whether or not the intellectual offspring is a phantom or a fertile truth. Socrates stresses that both he and actual midwives are barren, and cannot give birth to their own offspring. In spite of his own emptiness of ideas, Socrates claims to be skilled at bringing forth the ideas of others and examining them.

Dialectic: Socrates the Constructor

The method of dialectic is thought to be more Platonic than Socratic, though one can understand why many have associated it with Socrates himself. For one thing, the Greek dialegesthai ordinarily means simply "to converse" or "to discuss." Hence when Socrates is distinguishing this sort of discussion from rhetorical exposition in the Gorgias, the contrast seems to indicate his preference for short questions and answers as opposed to longer speeches.

There are two other definitions of dialectic in the Platonic corpus. First, in the Republic, Socrates distinguishes between dianoetic thinking, which makes use of the senses and assumes hypotheses, and dialectical thinking, which does not use the senses and goes beyond hypotheses to first principles. Second, in the Phaedrus, Sophist, Statesman, and Philebus, dialectic is defined as a method of collection and division. One collects things that are scattered into one kind and also divides each kind according to its species.

Some scholars view the elenchus and dialectic as fundamentally different methods with different goals, while others view them as consistent and reconcilable. Some even view them as two parts of one argument procedure, in which the elenchus refutes and dialectic constructs.

How Have Other Philosophers Understood Socrates?

Nearly every school of philosophy in antiquity had something positive to say about Socrates, and most of them drew their inspiration from him. Socrates also appears in the works of many famous modern philosophers. Immanuel Kant, the 18th century German philosopher best known for the categorical imperative, hailed Socrates, amongst other ancient philosophers, as someone who didn't just speculate but who lived philosophically. One of the more famous quotes about Socrates is from John Stuart Mill, the 19th century utilitarian philosopher who claimed that it is better to be a human being dissatisfied than a pig satisfied; better to be Socrates dissatisfied than a fool satisfied. The following is but a brief survey of Socrates as he is treated in philosophical thinking that emerges after the death of Aristotle in 322 BCE.

Hellenistic Philosophy

i. The Cynics

The Cynics greatly admired Socrates, and traced their philosophical lineage back to him. One of the first representatives of the Socratic legacy was the Cynic Diogenes of Sinope. No genuine writings of Diogenes have survived and most of our evidence about him is anecdotal. Nevertheless, scholars attribute a number of doctrines to him. He sought to undermine convention as a foundation for ethical values and replace it with nature. He understood the essence of human being to be rational, and defined happiness as freedom and self-mastery, an objective readily accessible to those who trained the body and mind.

ii. The Stoics

There is a biographical story according to which Zeno, the founder of the Stoic school and not the Zeno of Zeno's Paradoxes, became interested in philosophy by reading and inquiring about Socrates. The Stoics took themselves to be authentically Socratic, especially in defending the unqualified restriction of ethical goodness to ethical excellence, the conception of ethical excellence as a kind of knowledge, a life not requiring any bodily or external advantage nor ruined by any bodily disadvantage, and the necessity and sufficiency of ethical excellence for complete happiness.

Zeno is known for his characterization of the human good as a smooth flow of life. Stoics were therefore attracted to the Socratic elenchus because it could expose inconsistencies—both social and psychological—that disrupted one's life. In the absence of justification for a specific action or belief, one would not be in harmony with oneself, and therefore would not live well. On the other hand, if one held a position that survived cross-examination, such a position would be consistent and coherent. The Socratic elenchus was thus not just an important social and psychological test, but also an epistemological one. The Stoics held that knowledge was a coherent set of psychological attitudes, and therefore a person holding attitudes that could withstand the elenchus could be said to have knowledge. Those with inconsistent or incoherent psychological commitments were thought to be ignorant.

Socrates also figures in Roman Stoicism, particularly in the works of Seneca and Epictetus. Both men admired Socrates' strength of character. Seneca praises Socrates for his ability to remain consistent unto himself in the face of the threat posed by the Thirty Tyrants, and also highlights the Socratic focus on caring for oneself instead of fleeing oneself and seeking fulfilment by external means. Epictetus, when offering advice about holding to one's own moral laws as inviolable maxims, claims, "though you are not yet a Socrates, you ought, however, to live as one desirous of becoming a Socrates".

iii. The Skeptics

Broadly speaking, skepticism is the view that we ought to be either suspicious of claims to epistemological truth or at least withhold judgement from affirming absolute claims to knowledge. Amongst Pyrrhonian sceptics, Socrates appears at times like a dogmatist and at other times like a sceptic or inquirer. On the one hand, Sextus Empiricus lists Socrates as a thinker who accepts the existence of god and then recounts the cosmological argument that Xenophon attributes to Socrates. On the other hand, in arguing that human beings are impossible to conceive, Sextus Empiricus cites Socrates as unsure whether or not he is a human being or something else. Socrates is also said to have remained in doubt about this question.

Academic sceptics grounded their position that nothing can be known in Socrates' admission of ignorance in the Apology. Arcesilaus, the first head of the Academy to take it toward a skeptical turn, picked up from Socrates the procedure of arguing, first asking others to give their positions and then refuting them. While the Academy would eventually move away from skepticism, Cicero, speaking on behalf of the Academy of Philo, makes the claim that Socrates should be understood as endorsing the claim that nothing, other than one's own ignorance, could be known.

iv. The Epicurean

The Epicureans were one of the few schools that criticised Socrates, though many scholars think that this was in part because of their animus toward their Stoic counterparts, who admired him. In general, Socrates is depicted in Epicurean writings as a sophist, rhetorician, and sceptic who ignored natural science for the sake of ethical inquiries that concluded without answers. Colotes criticises Socrates' statement in the Phaedrus that he does not know himself, and Philodemus attacks Socrates' argument in the Protagoras that virtue cannot be taught.

The Epicureans wrote a number of books against several of Plato's Socratic dialogues, including the Lysis, Euthydemus, and Gorgias. In the Gorgias we find Socrates suspicious of the view that pleasure is intrinsically worthy and his insistence that pleasure is not the equivalent of the good. In defining pleasure as freedom from disturbance and defining this sort of pleasure as the sole good for human beings, the Epicureans shared little with the unbridled hedonism Socrates criticises Callicles for embracing. Indeed, in the Letter to Menoeceus, Epicurus explicitly argues against pursuing this sort of pleasure. Nonetheless, the Epicureans did equate pleasure with the good, and the view that pleasure is not the equivalent of the good could not have endeared Socrates to their sentiment.

Another reason for the Epicurean refusal to praise Socrates or make him a cornerstone of their tradition was his perceived irony. According to Cicero, Epicurus was opposed to Socrates' representing himself as ignorant while simultaneously praising others like Protagoras, Hippias, Prodicus, and Gorgias. This irony for the Epicureans was pedagogically pointless: if Socrates had something to say, he should have said it instead of hiding it.

v. The Peripatetics

Aristotle's followers, the Peripatetics, either said little about Socrates or were pointedly vicious in their attacks. Amongst other things, the Peripatetics accused Socrates of being a bigamist, a charge that appears to have gained so much traction that the Stoic Panaetius wrote a refutation of it. The general peripatetic criticism of Socrates, similar in one way to the Epicureans, was that he concentrated solely on ethics, and that this was an unacceptable ideal for the philosophical life.

How Socrates Influenced His World and the Future

A vast amount of literature has accumulated about Socrates, his personality, and his doctrine. And, nevertheless, in the history of philosophy, there is no person more mysterious than Socrates. The fact is that Socrates did not leave a written inheritance. People learn about his life and teachings mainly from the writings of his students and friends, including the philosopher Plato, and the historian Xenophon, or his ideological opponents, for example, the comedian Aristophanes, as well as from the books of later authors, including Aristotle. However, the attitude towards Socrates at different times was ambiguous, often diametrically opposite. Some of his contemporaries saw in him a dangerous atheist and sentenced him to death. Others considered the accusation of godlessness groundless and considered Socrates a deeply religious person. In subsequent times, up to the present day, Socrates was also evaluated and appreciated in different ways. For some, he is a great philosopher, for others, a boring moralist. Nevertheless, the fact remains undeniable that Socrates significantly influenced both his modernity and the future development of society, demonstrating his unsurpassed oratory, proposing his method of refuting statements, and making his splendid contribution to the development of philosophy and the transformation of social values.

References:

1. https://www.hellenicaworld.com/Greece/Person/en/BiasOfPriene.html
2. https://www.kalimera-greece.eu/greek-philosophers/bias-of-priene/
3. The Lives and Opinions of the Eminent Philosophers, by Diogenes Laertius
4. Pliny, 7, c. 33.
5. On-line version: [1] (http://classicpersuasion.org/pw/diogenes/)
6. https://ed-ubiquity.gsu.edu/wordpress/wp-content/uploads/2019/12/Ren%C3%A9e-Schatteman-Chilon-of-Sparta-proofs.pdf
7. https://www.sciencephoto.com/media/1199151/view/chilon-of-sparta-17th-century-illustration
8. https://manosgoing.com/cleobulus-of-lindos/
9. https://gretour.com/cleobulus-of-lindos/
10. https://theislandofrhodes.com/cleobulus-of-lindos/
11. 4.https://www.holidify.com/places/lindos/tomb-of-kleoboulous-sightseeing-1267747.html
12. https://www.hellenicaworld.com/Greece/Person/en/Periander.html
13. https://www.wikiwand.com/en/Periander
14. https://www.worldhistory.org/Periander/
15. https://military-history.fandom.com/wiki/Pittacus_of_Mytilene
16. https://engelsbergideas.com/portraits/pittacus-the-good-tyrant/
17. https://www.hellenicaworld.com/Greece/Person/en/PittacusOfMytilene.html
18. https://www.pbs.org/empires/thegreeks/background/4a_p1.html
19. https://www.greeka.com/greece-history/famous-people/solon/
20. https://www.historyskills.com/classroom/ancient-history/solon/

21. https://www.uvm.edu/~jbailly/courses/clas21/notes/atheniandemocracy.html
22. https://iep.utm.edu/thales/
23. https://www.thecollector.com/thales-miletus/
24. https://www.worldhistory.org/Thales_of_Miletus/
25. https://www.famousscientists.org/thales/
26. https://iep.utm.edu/anaximander/
27. https://www.famousscientists.org/anaximander/
28. https://www.thecollector.com/who-was-anaximander-9-facts/
29. https://www.thoughtco.com/biography-of-anaximander-1435033
30. https://iep.utm.edu/anaximenes/
31. https://www.worldhistory.org/Anaximenes/
32. https://www.drishtiias.com/blog/anaximander-and-anaximenes-the-other-two-milesians
33. https://astronomy.swin.edu.au/cosmos/a/Anaximenes
34. https://www.worldhistory.org/Xenophanes_of_Colophon/
35. https://www.lookingforwisdom.com/xenophanes/
36. https://classicalwisdom.com/philosophy/pre-socratics/xenophanes-singular-god/
37. https://chs.harvard.edu/chapter/11-xenophanes/
38. https://www.thecollector.com/heraclitus-philosopher-facts-you-should-know/
39. https://philosophyforchange.wordpress.com/2008/04/07/heraclitus-on-change/
40. https://www.thecollector.com/greek-philosopher-heraclitus-ephesus-quotes/
41. https://iep.utm.edu/heraclit/
42. https://iep.utm.edu/parmenid/
43. https://www.worldhistory.org/Parmenides/
44. https://www.worldhistory.org/article/175/parmenides--the-path-of-truth/
45. https://www.thecollector.com/parmenides-philosophy-facts-legacy/

46. https://www.lindahall.org/about/news/scientist-of-the-day/zeno-of-elea
47. https://www.thecollector.com/two-mind-blowing-paradoxes-by-zeno-of-elea
48. https://www.worldhistory.org/Zeno_of_Elea
49. https://platonicrealms.com/encyclopedia/Zeno-of-Elea
50. https://iep.utm.edu/zenos-paradoxes/
51. https://iep.utm.edu/empedocles
52. https://mathshistory.st-andrews.ac.uk/Biographies/Empedocles
53. https://www.worldhistory.org/Empedocles
54. https://www.famousscientists.org/empedocles
55. https://plato.stanford.edu/entries/anaxagoras/
56. https://www.encyclopedia.com/people/philosophy-and-religion/philosophy-biographies/anaxagoras
57. https://www.worldhistory.org/Anaxagoras/
58. https://www.newworldencyclopedia.org/entry/Anaxagoras
59. https://study.com/learn/lesson/atomism-theories-overview-leucippus.html
60. https://www.sparknotes.com/philosophy/presocratics
61. https://factsanddetails.com/world/cat56/sub401/entry-6207.html
62. https://www.thecollector.com/ancient-greeks-discover-atoms-atomism
63. https://iep.utm.edu/sophists
64. https://www.qcc.cuny.edu/socialsciences/ppecorino/intro_text/chapter%202%20greeks/sophists.htm
65. https://www.newworldencyclopedia.org/entry/Sophists
66. https://egyankosh.ac.in/bitstream/123456789/38071/1/Unit-3.pdf
67. https://penelope.uchicago.edu/Thayer/E/Gazetteer/Topics/philosophy/_Texts/COPHP/12*.html
68. https://www.britannica.com/biography/Socrates
69. https://iep.utm.edu/socrates/

70. https://plato.stanford.edu/entries/socrates/
71. https://www.history.com/topics/ancient-greece/socrates
72. https://www.worldhistory.org/socrates/
73. https://www.thecollector.com/socrates-philosophy-ancient-greek-philosopher-legacy

Bibliography:

1. Bias of Priene". Wikiquote. Wikiquote.org. Web. Retrieved on October 28, 2016.
2. Bias of Priene. Livius.org. Web. Retrieved on October 27, 2016.
3. Pleures, Konstantinos. The persecution of the best elements of society. Athens: Hilektron publications, 2013. Print.
4. Seven Sages Series: the wisdom of Bias of Priene. Baringtheaegis.blogspot.bg. July 7, 2015. Web. Retrieved on October 28, 2016.
5. "Pittacus". Helios New Encyclopaedic Dictionary. N.I. Luvaris, Passas, I. Athens: 1946. Print.
6. Ο Σοφότατος Πιττακός ο Μυτιληναίος. Ελλήνων Δίκτυο. Hellinon.net. Web. December 23, 2018.
7. Πλεύρης, Κωνσταντῖνος. Ὁ Διωγμὸς τῶν Ἀρίστων. Ἤλεκτρον. Ἀθῆναι: 2013. Print.

There is no path to **truth**. Nobody can lead you to **truth**. **Truth** is something that comes into being only when you know the art of listening and seeing, where there is love and compassion, and which has its own intelligence. Do not follow anybody spiritually. Do not obey. Have a free mind. Where there is freedom, there is love, and without freedom, one remains imprisoned.

Seeing the false as the false and the true as the true is transformation, because when you see something very clearly as the truth, that truth liberates. When you see that something is false, that false thing drops away. When you see that ceremonies are mere vain repetitions, when you see the truth of it and do not justify it, there is transformation, is there not?, because another bondage is gone. When you see that class distinction is false, that it creates conflict, creates misery, division between people - when you see the truth of it, that very truth liberates. The very perception of that truth is transformation, is it not? As we are surrounded by so much that is false, perceiving the falseness from moment to moment is transformation. Truth is not cumulative. It is from moment to moment. That which is cumulative, accumulated, is memory, and through memory you can never find truth, for memory is of time - time being the past, the present and the future. Time, which is continuity, can never find that which is eternal; eternity is not continuity. That which endures is not eternal. Eternity is in the moment. Eternity is in the now. The now is not the reflection of the past nor the continuance of the past through the present to the future.

— **J. Krishnamurti**

www.ingramcontent.com/pod-product-compliance
Lightning Source LLC
LaVergne TN
LVHW091544070526
838199LV00002B/199